OPEN TO THE SUN

A BILINGUAL ANTHOLOGY
OF LATIN-AMERICAN WOMEN POETS

Nora Jacquez Wieser
Editor

PERIVALE PRESS

©1979 on critical essays and English translations by Nora Jacquez Wieser

Library of Congress Catalog No. 78-78126

International Standard Book No. 0-912288-16-7

Typesetting by Freedmen's Organization

Printing by Gemini Graphics

Cover by Daniel Hayes

Published 1979 by
          PERIVALE PRESS
          13830 Erwin Street
          Van Nuys, California 91401

Distributed by   CAROLINE HOUSE PUBLISHERS, INC.

Third printing, 1982

CREDITS

A special note of acknowledgment for permission to use the original poems in Spanish to: Roy Beers Brannon, Doris Dana, Dr. María Matilde Meireles Correia Días, Olga Orozco, Editorial Universitaria/Universidad Nacional Autónoma de Nicaragua, Fondo de Cultura Económica de México, EDUCA de Costa Rica, Amanda Berenguer, Blanca Varela, Francisca Ossandón, Olga Elena Mattei, Nancy Bacelo, Belkis Cuza Malé, Rizzla B. de Pizarnik, Cristina Meneghetti

For
Eligio Jacquez
and
Juanita Córdova Jacquez
Fine parents

TABLE OF CONTENTS

MARÍA EUGENIA VAZ FERREIRA   8
    La voz del retorno   10
    The Voice of Return   11
    Historia póstuma   12
    Posthumous Story   13
    El ataúd flotante   14
    The Floating Casket   15
    Vaso furtivo   18
    A Furtive Glass   19
    La rima vacua   20
    The Vacuous Rime   21

DELMIRA AUGUSTINI   22
    Otra estirpe   24
    Another Race   25
    Visión   26
    Vision   27
    Lo inefable   30
    Unspeakable   31

ALFONSINA STORNI   32
    Peso ancestral   34
    Ancestral Weight   35
    La caricia perdida   36
    The Lost Caress   37
    Han venido   38
    They've Come   39
    Plaza en invierno   40
    The Park in Winter   41
    Voy a dormir   42
    I'm Going to Sleep   43

JUANA DE IBARBOUROU   44
    Vida-garfio   46
    Life Hook   47
    Crónica   48
    Chronicle   49

GABRIELA MISTRAL   50
    Los sonetos de la muerte I   52
    Death Sonnets I   53
    Los sonetos de la muerte II   54
    Death Sonnets II   55
    Los sonetos de la muerte III   56
    Death Sonnets III   57
    Pan   58
    Bread   59

CLAUDIA LARS   62
    Cartas escritas cuando crece la noche
        I   64
        III   66
        VI   68
        VIII   70
        X   72
        XI   74
        XIV   76
        XV   78
    Letters Written when Night Grows
        I   65
        III   67
        VI   69
        VIII   71
        X   73
        XI   75
        XIV   77
        XV   79

Evocación de Gabriela Mistral   80
Evocation of Gabriela Mistral   81

CECILIA MEIRELES   84
    Mar absoluto   86
    Absolute Sea   87

OLGA OROZCO   94
    Olga Orozco   96
    Olga Orozco   97
    Noica   98
    Noica   99
    Lamento de Jonás   100
    Jonah's Lament   101
    Esfinges suelen ser   104
    Sphinxes Inclined to be   105

THE NICARAGUAN GROUP   108
    Mariana Sanson
        "No he oído el golpe . . . "   110
        "I didn't hear the door . . . "   111
        "Cuando Dios estaba . . . "   112
        "When God was . . . "   113
    Lygia Guillén
        "una tristeza que me conocía . . . "   114
        "a sadness which already knew me . . . "   115
    Vidaluz Meneses
        Cuando yo me casé   116
        When I Married   117
        Advertencias   118
        Warnings   119
    Ana Ilce
        Mesa   120
        Table   121

Gioconda Belli
    Cotidiano   122
    The Mundane   123
Rosario Murillo
    Por culpa del retrato   124
    On Account of the Picture   125
Yolanda Blanco
    Llueve   126
    It's Raining   127

ROSARIO CASTELLANOS   128
    Elegía   130
    Elegy   131
    El otro   132
    Someone Else   133
    Amanecer   134
    Dawn   135
    Ajedrez   136
    Chess   137
    Se habla de Gabriel   138
    Speaking of Gabriel   139
    Meditación en el umbral   140
    Meditation on the Brink   141
    Lecciones de cosas   142
    Learning about Things   143

EUNICE ODIO   148
    "Escucha ese silencio . . . "   150
    "Listen to that silence . . . "   151
    Retratos del corazón   152
    Portraits of the heart   153

AMANDA BERENGUER   158
    Comunicaciones   160
    Communications   161

Tarea doméstica 164
Housework 165
Tabla del dos 166
The Two Times Table 167
Inventario solemne 168
Solemn Inventory 169
Poniente sobre el mar del sábado 4 de marzo 1972 172
The Sunset on the Sea, Saturday the 4th of March 1972 173
"El incendio se propaga . . . " 174
"The fire advances . . . " 174
(Poema cinético) 175

BLANCA VARELA 176
Madonna 178
Madonna 179
"Tal vez en primavera . . . " 180
"Perhaps in the spring . . . " 181
Vals del Ángelus I 182
The Waltz of the Angelus I 183
Vals del Ángelus II 184
The Waltz of the Angelus II 185

FRANCISCA OSSANDÓN 186
V 188
V 189
"Despliegue de cortezas . . . " 190
"The unfurling of bark . . . " 191
Juegos de la tierra y de la luz 192
Games of Earth and Light 193

OLGA ELENA MATTEI 194
"Yo soy una señora burguesa . . . " 196
"I am a bourgeois wife . . . " 197
"¿Recuerdas . . . " 200
"Do you remember . . . " 201

"Diciembre treinta y uno . . . "   202
"December thirty first . . . "   203
"Las galletas de soda . . . "   204
"Pairs . . . "   205
"Yo soy aquí . . . "   206
"I am here . . . "   207

NANCY BACELO   210
"No me interesan los datos . . . "   212
"I'm not interested in facts . . . "   213
Muy bajito   214
In a very, very quiet voice   215
"De vos de mí teñidos habitantes . . . "   216
"From you from me painted dwellers . . . "   217
"Me sorprendo en lugares . . . "   218
"I surprise myself in places . . . "   219
Todavía es temprano   220
It's still early   221

BELKIS CUZA MALÉ   222
Los Fotogénicos   224
The Photogenic Ones   225
Las Cenicientas   226
The Stepsisters   227
Oh, Mi Rimbaud   228
Oh, My Rimbaud   229
Mujer Brava Que se Casó Con Dios   230
The Shrew Who Married God   231
Fausto   232
Faust   233
Están Haciendo Una Muchacha Para la Epoca   234
They're Making a Girl for the Age   235

ALEJANDRA PIZARNIK   236
Pido el silencio   238
I ask silence   239

Antes 240
Before 241
Moradas 242
Abodes 243
Amantes 244
Lovers 245
Verde paraíso 246
Green Paradise 247
Crepúscielo 248
Dusk 249
Nombrarte 250
To Name You 251
Las Grandes Palabras 252
The Great Words 253
Fronteras inútiles 254
Useless Frontiers 255
Reloj 256
Clock 257
Fiesta 258
Party 259
Sortilegios 260
Sorceries 261

CRISTINA MENEGHETTI 262
 "la forma de dar forma al pensamiento . . . " 264
 "the utter form of giving form to thought . . . " 265
 "eran borrosos visitantes . . . " 266
 "they were nebulous visitors . . . " 267
 "la forma pequeña forma . . . " 268
 "the form small form . . . " 269
 "último capítulo de una madurez . . . " 270
 "the last chapter of maturity . . . " 271
 "te necesito . . . " 272
 "I need you . . . " 273

BIBLIOGRAPHY 274

xiii

INTRODUCTION

Pero puedo abrirme como una flor
y saltar desde los ojos para verme
abierta al sol.

But I can open myself like a flower
and jump down from my eyes to see me
open to the sun.

Eunice Odio
June 12, 1946
Granada, Nicaragua

Not too long ago I taught, for the first time, a class in the contemporary poetry of Latin America. I was intrigued by the fact that only a small amount of poetry by women was to be found in anthologies. Gabriela Mistral, Alfonsina Storni, and Delmira Augustini are the classic entries in a typical anthology otherwise dominated by male poets. Yet the poems by these women convinced me that a tradition had been established and there were more voices not being heard.

Not infrequently I would encounter a reference by a male critic to sentimentalism as a characteristic of womens' poetry; sentimentalism, especially defined as a doleful, languid expression of no poetic value and which only serves as an offensively intimate confession. Once I became more familiar with the topic of womens' poetry in Latin America, I realized that many of these women disliked the female term for poet ("poetisa"), preferring the masculine "poeta" because the former had acquired a negative connotation of sentimentality.

A primary goal for this anthology is to disprove the charge of sentimentality. Poems were deliberately selected which were not intimate confessions. Perhaps the one exception are the "Letters" by Claudia Lars. These poems, although confessions of a sort, have such an authentic honesty about them, they transcend their own source and express the ancient theme of rejection with universal resonance. The rest of the poetry

1

is characterized by a tremendous variety. We sought to include as many different styles of expression as possible. A second goal for the anthology is defined in terms of accessibility, that is to make accessible to the English reader, a wide variety of representative poetry from women in Latin America; and to make accessible to the Spanish reader some new or unknown poets who deserve recognition.

The anthology spans the 20th century with an emphasis on poetry written after 1950. Eleven of the poets are deceased; nine are living. Poets are included from Colombia, Perú, Chile, Brazil, Uruguay, Argentina, Costa Rica, Nicaragua, El Salvador, Cuba and Mexico. The book does not pretend to be exhaustive. There are many more fine poets who have not been included. In the case of some, such as Claribel Alegria from El Salvador or Nancy Morejón from Cuba, we were not able to see enough of their published poetry to make an adequate selection. Sometimes we would hear about a poet from other poets but could not find anything from their work still in print.

There are many factors which perpetuate the "out of print" or "not available" situation. The high cost of publishing results in limited copies. When the book is out of print, with rare exceptions, it remains so. Also, book distribution from one country to another in Latin America is such that only the relatively few established writers are known outside their own country. Often poets had heard of a poet from another country but they had never had access to the published work. Publishing cooperatives such as EDUCA in San José, Costa Rica, which serves six Central American Republics, can help in giving recognition to writers outside their country. But distribution of books is still a problem, basically an economic one.

Another factor detrimental to writers in many countries is direct or indirect censorship by the regime in power. Many Latin American regimes overtly ban particular books they deem offensive. These governments can exercise indirect censorship by creating obstacles or conditions which make writing impossible. In some countries the political situation is such that writers must direct all their energies to mere survival. This situation can make creative expression a somewhat superfluous luxury. There were instances where we felt almost apologetic trying to seek out women poets when the country itself teetered on the brink of social and economic disaster.

However, the reality that conditions are less than ideal for writers in much of Latin America does not dispense with another reality. Male writers have historically dominated the publishing scene. In poetry one

2

need only leaf through the contents of any anthology to find, under optimum conditions, the ratio of one woman to ten male poets. Interestingly enough women poets sometimes fare worse in anthologies compiled by male Hispanists from the United States. We can only conclude that there is a need for anthologies devoted exclusively to women poets in order to give them initial recognition. Only then will they have an equitable position at the starting point of literary posterity.

This anthology is not meant exclusively as a plaintive lament of the status quo. It seeks to present womens' views on themselves and their world as expressed in poetry. We can only fathom a more humane world if we understand our own historical reality. To this end, we cannot achieve worthwhile change if we don't try to know or understand how one half of humanity, namely women, think and feel.

Many times, the poets in this anthology are expressing the same themes as their male counterparts. Social protest poetry is very prevalent in Latin America. Poems by Cristian Meneghetti and Vidaluz Meneses reflect this protest. Meneghetti in "the last chapter of maturity" condemns the "do nothings" of the world who are too caught up in their own frivolities and lack the social concern necessary for change. Vidaluz Meneses' poem "Advertencias" (Warning) attacks the bureaucrat who has a distinct "Made in USA" image. The poem is a denouncement of cultural imperialism with an economic base; a denouncement frequently heard in Latin America and virtually ignored in the United States. Vidaluz Meneses is one of several excellent women poets from Nicaragua. We have simply identified them as The Nicaraguan Group.

One could postulate many theories for their existence in this small Central American Republic. One of these theories has a political base. The people have been subjected to almost half a century of strong-arm dictatorship by one ruling family. It is a country where all social classes have joined in protest. In the process it seems that women of the middle or upper class have taken stock of their lives and expressed themselves as never before. But poetry is not their only vehicle of expression; they are involved in political activities which often resulted in imprisonment or exile.

The contemporary English reader is familiar with another type of protest; the protest of the condition of women as expressed by women. In Latin America this protest, explicitly stated in poetry, is extremely rare. Three examples in the anthology are Rosario Castellanos' in "Lecciones de Cosas" (Learning about Things) and Alfonsina Storni in "Peso Ancestral" (Ancestral Weight) and "Han Venido" (They've Come). In the

3

Castellanos poem, the passivity of a woman is questioned. In Storni's "Ancestral Weight" the emotional burden of woman is revealed. In "They've Come" she depicts the transition of women from idealism to silent suffering.

In other poems perhaps the language of protest is not so explicit. But themes of women lie barely beneath the surface. We see their lives through their poetry. Poems such as "Inventario Solemne" (Solemn Inventory) by Amanda Berenguer, "Yo soy una señora burguesa" (I am a bourgeois wife) by Olga Elene Mattei, or "Cotidiano" (The Mundane) by Giaconda Belli provide insight into their world and have relevance for women everywhere. It is important to note that one aspect of womens' lives in Latin America is sacrosanct — the family and a woman's maternal role. We cannot envision a time in that society when the role of women as mothers will receive the scrutiny it currently undergoes in the United States. Certainly in these poems, the closest to scrutiny of motherhood is the poem by Rosario Castellanos "Hablando de Gabriel" (Speaking of Gabriel). But the poem concludes with a positive spirit of giving, and receiving, in turn, a purpose for living.

The reader will find in the anthology two poems with the same theme treated very differently. Examples are Cecilia Meireles' "Mar Absoluto" (Absolute Sea) and Gabriela Mistral's "Pan" (Bread). The theme for both these poems might be termed the revelation of the poetic self through a historical past. Meireles uses the symbol of the sea to speak of herself and her ancestors. It is a symbol often used by male poets, and Meireles gives the symbol special meaning as a powerful cyclical force. Gabriela Mistral's poem places herself in history through the image of bread, a symbol which has both female significance and a Christian precedent. It is difficult to state categorically the extent to which the poems are affected by a woman's particular sensitivity. However it would be interesting to do a comparative study of poems with a similar theme by male poets. Studies such as this would support the importance of recognizing women writers to achieve a needed balance in literature, if it is an expression of all humans' concerns.

To speak of poetic generations or schools in this poetry is difficult. Some of the women have incorporated themselves into particular movements in their country. Olga Orozco and her work in surrealism is an example. But after meeting scores of women poets on trips to South America, Central America, Cuba and Mexico, my conclusion is that the majority of these women write independently of movements. Many of them spoke to me of writing poetry as something they needed to do to externalize profound inner feelings. This is not to say that they are uninformed about better known movements or poets. The works of English and U.S. poets are often known through efforts such as that of Elizabeth Azcona Cranwell of Argentina who has completed the Spanish translation of Dylan Thomas's poems. Dr. Beth Miller, a United States Hispanist, has compiled a small book of U.S. women poets (Wakoski, Rich, Sexton, Plath among others) in Spanish translation and published in Mexico. Ironically, these foreign writers will sometimes receive wider recognition than the countries' own authors. But poets such as César Vallejo of Peru and Miguel Hernández of Spain are almost universally appreciated.

In many countries there are small poetry journals often compiled by younger poets as a publishing outlet. Some countries have poetry workshops where young poets gather to read and discuss poetry, usually under the guidance of an older, more experienced mentor. I remember one such workshop in San José, Costa Rica under the direction of the poets Julieta Dobles and Laureano Albán. The young participants would read their work. Then the group would have a very ritualistic procedure to determine one of three fates for the work: it needed more effort; it should be discarded, or it was accepted. The only two women in the group seemed very shy about the reading of their work, almost as if it exposed embarrassing feelings.

Who are the women that write poetry? They are overwhelmingly, white, middle or upper class. If there are Indian or Black women involved in poetry, it is probably in the manner of oral tradition which hopefully we can learn from anthropologists. Until now the voices of Indian or Black women writers in the mainstream of literature are virtually unknown.

The women who write poetry work at different jobs which range from teaching to writing astrology columns. Some have families who demand a great deal of time. A few are playing a vital role in the cultural life of their country. Perhaps the outstanding example is Nancy Bacelo in Uruguay who is motivated by the concept of art as accessible to all people. Her organization of Uruguay's National Book Fair is an outgrowth of this belief.

For all of the women in this anthology poetry is and has been a serious medium for expression. They have worked diligently at perfecting their art. In Alejandra Pizarnik's introduction we can read her own words

5

describing the exacting creative process. We can follow the evolution of Amanda Berenguer's poetry as her mind incessantly explores new possibilities for communication.

In conclusion this book will have served its purpose if a vast chasm has been created between sentimentality and Latin American Women's poetry, so that the two terms cease to be synonomous in the minds of readers, publishers and critics. In reading the poems by these women, we learn of their world, often painful, despairing, tinged with suicides and other tragedies. But sometimes it is joyful, idealistic and certainly always probing the very roots of existence. They are women from another culture speaking to us in womens' language, and, in the end telling us a great deal about ourselves.

I wish to thank my students at Oberlin College who encouraged and worked on this book, especially Leslie Keffer, Priscilla Joslin, Marti Moody and Susan Pensak. I assume full responsibility for the translations since they were done by myself and my students under my direction. The exceptions are Dr. Maureen Ahern's translations of Rosario Castellanos and Dr. Darlene J. Sadlier's translations of Cecilia Meireles. I want to acknowledge my family's role because they tapped hitherto unknown resources for survival during my periods of research. My thanks to Oberlin College for providing grants which made the research possible. I also want to thank David St. John, Dr. Terisa Turner, Amanda Berenguer and José Pedro Díaz for their careful reading of the manuscript and their helpful suggestions. Lastly, to all the women poets I met, thank you warmly for the learning experience.

Nora Jacquez Wieser
Oberlin College

María Eugenia Vaz Ferreira
Uruguay
1875–1924

EVEN BEFORE THE POETRY of Delmira Augustini was known, another Uruguayan, a quiet, retiring young woman, was writing poetry for newspapers and journals. She had poetry published as early as 1895 but was overcome by illness before her work could be organized in book form. After her death, her brother published a slim volume which is her only book of poems. In a note to the edition he speaks of the uncertainty of the chronological ordering of the poems and other difficulties of the editing task which he could not resolve before his sister's death. In 1975 the National Library of Montevideo published a bibliography of her work in commemoration of the 100th anniversary of her birth. This bibliography will undoubtedly help further studies in her poetry since it is virtually unknown outside of her country. Yet historically she plays an important role in women's poetry in Latin America because she is a predecessor of the four "classic" women poets, Delmira Augustini, Juana de Ibarbourou, Alfonsina Storni and Gabriela Mistral.

Her poetry is characterized by a delicate musicality which is reminiscent of the early modernist poet Manuel Gutiérrez Nájera of Mexico. She creates a semi-dream world of the night, mirages, crystal birds; yet we do not find the sumptuous exoticism of the early Ruben Darío, the Messiah of the Modernist movement in the Spanish-speaking world. The tone of her poetry is predominantly melancholy. A resignation to suffering is evident. There is never protest. Death is almost welcomed as we see in the poem "The Floating Casket." This poem is a forerunner of the nearly macabre themes that we will later find in some of Gabriela Mistral's poetry.

Adolfo Silva Delgado, Director of the National Library in Uruguay, says that her poetry is linked to the vital impulses of a woman, at the beginning of the century who wanted to be and indeed, was, more than was possible within the prevailing rigidity of the social atmosphere.[1]

Books of Poetry

La Isla de los Cánticos   1924

---

1. Adolfo Silva Delgado, *Bibliografía María Eugenia Vaz Ferreira* (Montevideo: Biblioteca Nacional, 1975), p. 9.

VOZ DEL RETORNO

Nada le queda al náufrago; ya nada: ni siquiera
la dulce remembranza de un viejo sueño vano,
ni la marchita y frágil ala de una quimera
que al estrecharse deja su polvo entre la mano.
La media noche es tarde y el alba fué temprano,
y el orgulloso día le dijo al sol: "Espera";
Quien sin besarla aspira la flor de Primavera,
pasa como una sombra por el jardín humano.

Violetas de los prados en el solar fragante,
rosas de los pensiles rojas y perfumadas
que al pasajero abrieron su misterioso broche;
el náufrago retorna como una sombra errante,
sin una sola estrella de flámulas doradas
con qué alumbrar el fondo de su infinita noche.

La Isla des los Cánticos

THE VOICE OF RETURN

Nothing remains from the shipwrecked survivor; nothing:
   not even
the sweet memory of a futile old illusion,
nor the crumpled and fragile wing of a fantasy
which, when stretched, leaves its dust on the hand.
Midnight is late and dawn was early,
and the proud day said to the sun: "Wait";
He who wishes for the spring flower without kissing it,
passes like a shadow through the human garden.

Meadow violets in the fragrant sun,
Red perfumed roses in the garden
opened their secret brooches to the traveler;
the shipwrecked survivor returns like an errant shadow
without a single gilded star
to light the base of his infinite night.

Translated by Nora Wieser
La Isla de los Cánticos

HISTORIA PÓSTUMA

Todo me lo diste, todo:
el ritmo azul de las cunas
en cuentos maravillosos
glosados de suaves músicas . . .

Las palabras melodiosas
divinas como el silencio,
las rosas de nieve y oro
perfumadas de secretos . . .

Las albas anunciadoras
de los venturosos días
henchidos de primaveras
refulgentes de sonrisas . . .

Las pálidas nebulosas
de los cielos taciturnos,
la soledad, el olvido
y la paz de los sepulcros.

La Isla de los Cánticos

POSTHUMOUS STORY

You gave me everything
the blue rhythm of cradles
in fantasy bedtime tales
glossed with gentle music . . .

Melodious words
divine like silence,
Gold and snow roses
perfumed with secrets . . .

Dawns as messengers
of good days
swollen with springtimes
resplendent with smiles . . .

The nebulous pallor
of taciturn skies,
alone, oblivion
and the quiet of tombs.

Translated by Nora Wieser
La Isla de los Cánticos

EL ATAÚD FLOTANTE

Mi esperanza, yo sé que tú estás muerta.
No tienes de los vivos
más que la instable fluctuación perpetua;
no sé si un tiempo vigorosa fuiste,
ahora, estás muerta.
Te han roído quién sabe
qué larvas metafísicas que hicieron
entre tu dulce carne su cosecha.
En vano
el mágico abanico de tus alas
con irisadas ráfagas me orea
soltando al aire turbadoras chispas.
Yo sé que tú eres de esas
que vuelven redivivas en la noche
a decir otra vez su último verbo . . .
Yo te he visto venir
blanca y piadosa como un santo espíritu
sobre el vaivén de las marinas ondas;
te he visto en el fulgor de las estrellas,
y hasta los bordes de mi quieta planta
danzan tus llamas en festivas rondas.
Pero si al interior vuelvo los ojos
veo la sombra de tu mancha negra,
miro tu nebulosa en el vacío
dar poco a poco su visión suspensa;
sin el miraje de los fuegos fatuos
veo la sombra de tu mancha negra.
No llores porque sé; los ojos míos
saben vivir en lontananzas huecas;
míralos secos y tranquilos; márchate
y el flotante ataúd reposar deja

THE FLOATING CASKET

My hope, I know you're dead.
From the living, you have
no more than the unstable, perpetual fluctuation;
I don't know if you were alive at one time,
now, you are dead.
Who knows what metaphysical larvae
have gnawed at you
and made their harvest
from your sweet flesh.
In vain
the magic fan of your wings
refreshes me with multi-hued breezes,
disturbing sparks left in the air.
I know you are one of those
who return revived at night
to say their last word . . .
I've seen you come before,
pious, white like a holy spirit
on the movement of the waves.
I've seen you in the brilliance of the stars
and even the edges of my quiet soles
dance your flames in festive rounds.
But if I turn my eyes inside
I see the shadow of your black stain
I see your nebulous self in the emptiness
gradually, your suspended vision
without the mirage of foolish vigor,
I see the shadow of your black stain.
Don't cry because I know; my eyes
can live with hollow distances;
see them now, calm, dry; go away
and let the floating casket rest

hasta que junto a tí también tendida
nos abracemos como hermanas buenas
y otra vez enlazadas nos durmamos
en el sepulcro vivo de la tierra.

La Isla de los Cánticos

until, lying next to you
we embrace as good sisters
and once again united we sleep
in earth's living tomb.

Translated by Nora Wieser
La Isla de los Cánticos

VASO FURTIVO

Por todo lo breve y frágil,
superficial, fugitivo,
por lo que no tiene bases,
argumentos ni principios;
por todo lo que es liviano,
veloz, mudable y finito;
por las volutas del humo,
por las rosas de los tirsos,
por la espuma de las olas
y las brumas del olvido . . .
por lo que les carga poco
a los pobres peregrinos
de esta trashumante tierra
grave y lunática, brindo
con palabras transitorias
y con vaporosos vinos
de burbujas centelleantes
en cristales quebradizos . . .

La Isla de los Cánticos

A FURTIVE GLASS

To all that is brief and fragile
superficial, unstable,
To all that lacks foundation
argument or principles;
To all that is light,
fleeting, changing, finite
To smoke spirals,
wand roses,
To sea foam
and mists of oblivion . . .
To all that is light in weight
for itinerants
on this transient earth
Somber, raving,
with transitory words
and vaporous bubbly wines
I toast
in breakable glasses . . .

Translated by Nora Wieser
La Isla de los Cánticos

LA RIMA VACUA

   Grito de sapo
llega hasta mí de las nocturnas charcas . . .
la tierra está borrosa y las estrellas
me han vuelto las espaldas.

   Grito de sapo, mueca
de la armonía, sin tono, sin eco,
llega hasta mí de las nocturnas charcas . . .

La vaciedad de mi profundo hastío
rima con él el dúo de la nada.

La Isla de los Cánticos

THE VACUOUS RIME

The scream of a frog
comes to me from night ponds . . .
the earth is dulled and the stars
have turned their back on me.

The scream of a frog, wry face
of harmony, no tone, no echo,
it comes to me from night ponds . . .
The hollow of my profound weariness
rimes with it, the duo of nothing.

Translated by Nora Wieser
La Isla de los Cánticos

Delmira Augustini
Uruguay
1886–1914

DELMIRA AUGUSTINI WAS THE ONLY daughter of a middle class family in
Montevideo. She was called "La Nena" (the child) by her adoring parents.
The family would often be seen out for a stroll, pausing to feed the
pigeons from a park bench. They were sometimes a target for the curious,
this seemingly innocent family. The reason was the poetry that "La Nena"
was writing and publishing. Never before had the Spanish speaking world
heard such unabashedly erotic poetry from a woman.

Alberto Zum Felde, the great Uruguayan critic, in the prologue to
her complete works speaks to this eroticism: "Those who take Delmira
Augustini for an erotic poet in the usual sense of the word will not under-
stand her . . . She has a constant evasion of reality and the world, a
desperate search for the ideal form of her Desire, a transcending of a
transworld and a super reality, in whose secret night the superhuman
images of her dream world ignite like stars of the abyss. Her eroticism
burns and consumes itself, a burning bramble in the desert of a place
beyond flesh and life."

On the other hand, another Uruguayan critic, Arturo Sergio Visca,
sees the work of Augustini enveloped in two myths, one vital and the other
aesthetic. He negates a metaphysical anguish. He says: "In Delmira
Augustini's poetry there is no metaphysics, mysticism or religiosity: there
is only an ardent erotic-vital intoxication. This is articulated by the pro-
found poetic I, with a real life and inner experience which has often been
denied her, creating the false problem of how a poetic world could be

constructed which is foreign to all experience in reality."[1] Nonetheless, the controversy, which continues, seemingly cannot negate the impact of her poetry. Some of her finest work is found in her third book *Los Cálices Vacíos* (The Empty Chalices).

She was married in August 1913 to Enrique Job Reyes, a somewhat dull man who had been courting her for five years. The marriage lasted twenty one days before Delmira left him and returned to the family home, the protection of her dominating mother and doting father. However, she continued to see Reyes secretly and in one of these encounters he killed her and took his own life.

Today in a dusty cupboard of a back room in the National Library in Montevideo, Delmira's wedding dress hangs forlornly next to her favorite doll who sits staring rigidly at the curious with one eye closed in a perpetual wink.

Books of Poetry

El Libro Blanco	1907
Cantos de la Mañana	1910
Los Cálices Vacíos	1913
El Rosario de Eros	
Los Astros del Abismo	Posthumous

La Alborada (1896–1904) Appeared in the official 1940 edition of her poetry

---

1. Arturo Sergio Visca, *Ensayos Sobre Literatura Uruguaya* (Montevideo: Comisión Nacional de Homenaje del sesquicentenario de los Hechos Históricos de 1825, 1975) p. 214.

OTRA ESTIRPE

Eros, yo quiero guiarte, Padre Ciego . . .
Pido a tus manos todopoderosas
¡su cuerpo excelso derramado en fuego
sobre mi cuerpo desmayado en rosas!

La eléctrica corola que hoy despliego
brinda el nectario de un jardín de Esposas;
para sus buitres en mi carne entrego
todo un enjambre de palomas rosas.

Da a las dos sierpes de su abrazo, crueles,
mi gran tallo febril . . . Absintio, mieles,
viérteme de sus venas, de su boca . . .

¡Así tendida soy el surco ardiente
donde puede nutrirse la simiente
de otra Estirpe sublimemente loca!

Los Cálices Vacíos

ANOTHER RACE

Eros, blind father, I want to guide you.
I ask this at your invulnerable hands:
May his magnificent body be poured out
—in flames!—
over mine, pale and limp among the roses.

Today, I'll unfold my own electric petals.
I'll offer him the nectar
from a whole garden of wives.
I'll draw his vultures to my flesh,
send him a swarm of pink doves.

They give him my great stem, my fevered leaves;
they give me to the two cruel snakes
that live in his embrace.
Wormwood and honey
spill in me from his veins, his mouth . . .

Stretched out like this, I'm a hot furrow
where the seed of another race
can feed itself, the seed
of a race that's sublimely insane!

Translated by Marti Moody
Los Cálices Vacíos

VISIÓN

¿Acaso fue en un marco de ilusión,
en el profundo espejo del deseo,
o fue divina y simplemente en vida
que yo te vi velar mi sueño la otra noche?
En mi alcoba agrandada de soledad y miedo,
taciturno a mi lado apareciste
como un hongo gigante, muerto y vivo,
brotado en los rincones de la noche,
húmedos de silencio,
y engrasados de sombra y soledad.

Te inclinabas a mí, supremamente,
como a la copa de cristal de un lago
sobre el mantel de fuego del desierto;
te inclinabas a mí, como un enfermo
de la vida a los opios infalibles
y a las vendas de piedra de la Muerte.

Te inclinabas a mí como el creyente
a la oblea de cielo de la hostia . . .
-Gota de nieve con sabor de estrellas
que alimenta los lirios de la carne,
chispa de Dios que estrella los espíritus-.
Te inclinabas a mí como el gran sauce
de la Melancolía
a las hondas lagunas del silencio;
te inclinabas a mí como la torre
de mármol del Orgullo,
minada por un monstruo de tristeza,
a la hermana solemne de su sombra . . .
Te inclinabas a mí como si fuera
mi cuerpo la inicial de tu destino
en la página oscura de mi lecho;
te inclinabas a mí como al milagro
de una ventana abierta al más allá.

VISION

Maybe all I saw was the mirror
of my desires, an illusory
frame around it all . . .
Or it's simply a miracle: did I really
see you the other night, watching me sleep?
Loneliness and terror had made my bedroom
huge; you appeared at my side
like a giant fungus, both dead and alive,
in the corners of the night,
damp with silence,
greased with solitude and darkness.

You leaned toward me, utterly
toward me — as toward the lake, the crystal cup
on the desert's tablecloth.
You leaned toward me as an invalid
leans toward the drugs that won't fail him,
toward the stone bandages of death.

You leaned toward me as a believer
toward the blessed communion wafer —
the snowflake that tastes
of stars, nourishing the lilies of man's flesh;
God's spark, a star for man.
You leaned toward me as sadness, the large willow,
leans toward silence, its deep pools.
You leaned toward me like pride's tower,
its marble quarried by the monster sadness,
leaning toward its own shadow, its great sister.
You leaned toward me as if my body
in this dark page of a bed
was where your destiny began.
You leaned toward me as toward a window looking out
upon whatever follows death.

¡Y te inclinabas más que todo eso!

Y era mi mirada una culebra
apuntada entre zarzas de pestañas,
al cisne reverente de tu cuerpo.
Y era mi deseo una culebra
glisando entre los riscos de la sombra
a la estatua de lirios de tu cuerpo.
Tú te inclinabas más y más . . . y tanto,
y tanto te inclinaste,
que mis flores eróticas son dobles,
Toda tu vida se imprimió en mi vida . . .

Yo esperaba suspensa el aletazo
del abrazo magnífico; un abrazo
de cuatro brazos que la gloria viste
de fiebre y de milagro; ¡será un vuelo!
Y pueden ser los hechizados brazos
cuatro raíces de una raza nueva.

Yo esperaba suspensa el aletazo
del abrazo magnífico . . .
                                    Y cuando
te abrí los ojos como un alma, vi
¡que te hacías atrás y te envolvías
en yo no sé qué pliegue inmenso de la sombra!

Los Cálices Vacíos

28

And you leaned even more!

My vision was a snake
aimed through eyelashes of brambles
toward your body, oh reverent swan.
And my lust was a snake
gliding through dark canyons
toward your body, oh statue of lilies.
You leaned farther and farther, and so far,
you leaned so far,
that my sexual flowers grew to twice their size
and my star has been larger since then.
Your whole life was imprinted on mine.

Anxious, uncertain, I waited
for the rustling wings that signal a magnificent embrace,
a miraculous and passionate embrace,
an embrace of four arms; flight!
The enchanted arms can be
four roots of a new race.

Anxious, uncertain, I waited
for the rustling wings that signal a magnificent embrace . . .
                              And when
I opened my eyes — like a soul — to you:
I saw you'd fallen back, you were wrapped
in some huge fold of darkness!

Translated by Marti Moody
Los Cálices Vacíos

LO INEFABLE

Yo muero extrañamente . . . No me mata la Vida,
no me mata la Muerte, no me mata el Amor;
muero de un pensamiento mudo como una herida . . .
¿No habéis sentido nunca el extraño dolor

de un pensamiento inmenso que se arraiga en la vida,
devorando alma y carne y no alcanza a dar flor?
¿Nunca llevasteis dentro una estrella dormida
que os abrasaba enteros y no daba un fulgor?

¡Cumbre de los Martirios! . . . ¡Llevar eternamente,
desgarradora y árida, la trágica simiente
clavada en las entrañas como un diente feroz! . . .

Pero arrancarla un día en una flor que abriera
milagrosa, inviolable . . . ¡Ah, más grande no fuera
tener entre las manos la cabeza de Dios!

Cantos de la Mañana

UNSPEAKABLE^(s)

The way I die is strange . . . It's not life
that kills me, not death, not love.
I die of thought that's silent, like a wound.
Haven't you felt the pain

of a huge thought? One rooted like a plant
in your life, that gobbles soul and meat
but will not flower.
Haven't you carried, inside you,
a sleeping star,
that consumes you but will not shine?

This is martyrdom! To carry
forever a barren and tragic seed.
nailed, like a tooth, in your organs.

But what if you yank it out one day and find
an inviolate flower
that will never die . . .
It couldn't be more wonderful
to hold God's head in your hands.

Translated by Marti Moody
Cantos de la Mañana

Alfonsina Storni
Argentina
1892–1938

ALFONSINA STORNI CAME TO Buenos Aires from the provinces where she
had worked as a school teacher. 1916 marks the date of publication of
her first book of poetry and also the date of her inauguration into the
literary life of Buenos Aires. In addition to poetry, she wrote short novels,
stories and dramas. Some of the latter were presented in Buenos Aires
between 1926 and 1938. Under a pseudonym she did articles of criticism
for "La Nación," an important Argentine newspaper.

She won several important poetry prizes in Argentina. Today she is
perhaps best remembered for her feminist poetry. Some of this poetry
becomes a bitter denouncement of men and the subordinate role they
assign to women. It is commonly believed that her bitterness was due to
a personal experience of rejection. One can sense, however, a broader,
more historical perspective in poems such as "They've Come" or "Ancestral
Weight."

She herself preferred her later poetry at the end of her life. This
poetry is much more subdued or not concerned at all with the social role
of women. There are frequent themes of the sea and its landscapes or of
the sterility of the city. In 1938, the year of her death, she wrote the pro-
logue for an anthology of her poetry published by Espasa-Calpe. In this

prologue she says ". . . it is not out of place to say that I have some prefer-
ence for my work that begins with OCRE (1925) and a preference for the
poems in the last pages of this selection, which I know is against the
majority opinion . . . As much as I denounce my initial style, overcharged
with romantic honeys, I must nevertheless recognize that I had in hand the
critical position, a fact universally diffused, of a 20th century woman
facing the grip, still sweet, but simultaneously getting colder, of a patriar-
chal system."

Her conscience as a writer is evidenced as her prologue continues:
"But to go back when the pen has already drained (the theme) is equal to
living by plagarizing oneself primarily because one accent reached the
majority . . . The worst that can happen to a poet is that he is forced to
imitate himself."

Incurably ill, Alfonsina Storni drowned herself in the sea on October
24, 1938.

Books of Poetry

La Inquietud del Rosal	1916
El Dulce Daño	1918
Irremediablemente	1919
Languidez	1920
Ocre	1925
Mundo de Siete Pozos	1934
Poesías (after 1934)	

PESO ANCESTRAL

Tú me dijiste: no lloró mi padre;
tú me dijiste: no lloró mi abuelo;
no han llorado los hombres de mi raza,
eran de acero.

Así diciendo te brotó una lágrima
y me cayó en la boca . . . más veneno.
Yo no he bebido nunca en otro vaso
así pequeño.

Débil mujer, pobre mujer que entiende,
dolor de siglos conocí al beberlo:
Oh, el alma mía soportar no puede
todo su peso.

El Dulce Daño

ANCESTRAL WEIGHT

You said: *My father didn't cry.*
You said: *My grandfather didn't cry.*
The men of my family
never cried. They were like steel.

Saying this you
shed a tear.
It fell in my mouth, more poison.
I've never drunk from a cup
so small.

Frail woman, poor woman
who understands,
I drank centuries of pain
in your tear, and my
soul just can't bear
all that weight.

Translated by Marti Moody
El Dulce Daño

LA CARICIA PERDIDA

Se me va de los dedos la caricia sin causa,
se me va de los dedos . . . En el viento, al rodar,
la caricia que vaga, sin destino ni objeto,
la caricia perdida, ¿quién la recogerá?

Pude amar esta noche con piedad infinita;
pude amar al primero que acertara a llegar.
Nadie llega. Están solos los floridos senderos.
La caricia perdida, rodará . . . rodará.

Si en el viento te llaman esta noche, viajero,
si estremece las ramas un dulce suspirar,
si te oprime los dedos una mano pequeña
que te toma y te deja, que te logra y se va.

Si no ves esa mano, ni la boca que besa,
si es el aire quien teje la ilusión de llamar,
oh viajero, que tienes como el cielo los ojos,
en el viento fundida ¿me reconocerás?

Languidez

THE LOST CARESS

There's no call for the caress that leaves my fingers,
there's no call . . . Who'll pick up
a wandering caress that rolls
in the wind, with no destination
and no place to go, the lost caress . . .

Tonight I could love
with infinite compassion, I could love the first person
who happened by. No one comes.
The paths, the flowers: alone.
The lost caress will wander aimlessly.

If something in the wind, traveler,
calls out to you tonight,
if a sweet breath shakes the branches,
if a small hand presses your fingers and it
catches you and leaves,
grabs you and moves off; if you don't

See that hand, or the mouth
kissing you, if the air
weaves the illusion of a call . . .
Oh traveler, you with your eyes like the sky,
when the wind's been melted down
will you recognize me there?

Translated by Marti Moody
Languidez

HAN VENIDO

Hoy han venido a verme
mi madre y mis hermanas.

Hace ya tiempo que yo estaba sola
con mis versos, mi orgullo; en suma, nada.

Mi hermana, la más grande, está crecida:
es rubiecita; por sus ojos pasa
el primer sueño. He dicho a la pequeña:
-*La vida es dulce. Todo mal acaba . . .*

Mi madre ha sonreído como suelen
aquellos que conocen bien las almas;
ha puesto sus dos manos en mis hombros,
Me ha mirado muy fijo . . .
        Y han saltado mis lágrimas.

Hemos comido juntas en la pieza
más tibia de la casa.
Cielo primaveral . . . ; para mirarlo
fueron abiertas todas las ventanas.

Y mientras conversábamos tranquilas
de tantas cosas viejas y olvidadas,
mi hermana, la menor, ha interrumpido:
-*Las golondrinas pasan . . .*

                              Languidez

THEY'VE COME

Today my mother and sisters
have come to see me.

For some time I'd been alone
with my verses, my pride; in short, nothing.

My sister, the older one, has grown up,
still slight and fair; the first dream passes
through her eyes. I've said to the little one:
Life is sweet. What's bad goes away . . .

My mother smiles, as those who know souls
are accustomed to smile.
She puts her two hands on my shoulders,
she looks at me very steadily . . .
                    I burst into tears.

We've eaten together, in the most
lived-in room of the house.
A springlike sky . . . All the windows open
so we could see it.

And as we talk, we tranquil women,
of so many old and forgotten things,
my sister, the younger one, interrupts:
The swallows are passing . . .

Translated by Marti Moody
Languidez

PLAZA EN INVIERNO

Árboles desnudos
corren una carrera
por el rectángulo de la plaza.
En sus epilépticos esqueletos
de volcadas sombrillas
se asientan,
en bandada compacta,
los amarillos
focos luminosos.

Bancos inhospitalarios,
húmedos,
expulsan de su borde
a los emigrantes soñolientos.
Oyendo fáciles arengas ciudadanas,
un prócer,
inmóvil sobre una columna,
se hiela en su bronce.

Mundo de Siete Pozos

THE PARK IN WINTER

Naked trees
run a race
around the square's rectangle.
Capsized shadows
adjust themselves
in the epileptic skeletons,
yellow, luminous
lights in a covey.

Damp,
inhospitable benches
reject drowsy emigrants
from their borders.
Overhearing the talk of the town,
some noble official,
quiet on a column,
is freezing in his bronze.

Translated by Nora Wieser
Mundo de Siete Pozos

VOY A DORMIR

Dientes de flores, cofia de rocío,
manos de hierbas, tú, nodriza fina,
ténme prestas las sábanas terrosas
y el edredón de musgos escardados.

Voy a dormir, nodriza mía, acuéstame.
Ponme una lámpara a la cabecera;
una constelación; la que te guste;
todas son buenas; bájala un poquito.
Déjame sola: oyes romper los brotes . . .
te acuna un pie celeste desde arriba
y un pájaro te traza unos compases

para que olvides . . . Gracias. ¡Ah, un encargo!
Si él llama nuevamente por teléfono,
le dices que no insista, que he salido.

(Escrito pocas horas antes de su muerte)

42

I'M GOING TO SLEEP

With flowers for teeth, a hairnet of dew,
hands made of grass—you, fine nurse,
have the earthen sheets ready for me,
and the eiderdown of weeded moss.

I'm going to sleep, nurse; put me to bed.
Place a lamp by the headboard for me—
a constellation, one you like.
They're all fine; lower it a bit . . .

Leave me alone. You hear the buds of trees
breaking. Above you a heavenly foot
wedges you on earth, a bird
is tracing patterns in the sky
so you'll forget . . . Thank you . . . Oh, one last thing:
if he phones again tell him
not to insist, that I've left.

(Written a few hours before her death)
Translated by Marti Moody

43

Juana de Ibarbourou

Uruguay

1897-1979

IN 1919 A BOOK ENTITLED *LAS LENGUAS DE DIAMANTE* (Diamond Tongues) appeared. It was an immediate success and Juana de Ibarbourou, the author, was known throughout the Spanish-speaking world because her poetry spoke of loving and being loved with a freshness and vigor unknown in Spanish letters. She became even more famous with two subsequent books. She gave generously of herself and her talents, writing prologues for other aspiring poets.

In her early poems the will to live is channeled into the act of loving. Love, then, is a constant well spring, a renewal of life. On the other hand there is the frequent theme of mortal flesh which is often terrifying for the poet because love ends and therefore, life ceases. In her later poems, there is a religious theme which makes her tone more subdued, more resigned. The two poems, "Life-Hook" and "Chronicle" illustrate the two extremes of her poetry world: zest for life and disillusionment. Her book *PÉRDIDA* (Lost) published in 1950, speaks of the effects of time on her illusions.

Yet Juana de Ibarbourou and her love poetry achieved almost mythical proportions. On the negative side, a host of unsuccessful imitators sprang up among the women poets; there are still imitators, conscious or otherwise. The result is a banal sentimentality which has been detrimental to good poetry by women in Latin America. Critics, all too often, have never looked at women's poetry beyond this negative influence of Ibarbourou's early poems.

Juana de Ibarbourou lived her last years virtually isolated, an old and sick woman in Montevideo, a strong contrast to her years of travel and acclaim when she was known as "Juana of America."

Books of Poetry

Las Lenguas de Diamante	1919
Raíz Salvaje	1922
La Rosa de los Vientos	1930
Perdida	1950
Azor	1953

VIDA-GARFIO

Amante: no me lleves, si muero, al camposanto.
A flor de tierra abre mi fosa, junto al riente
alboroto divino de alguna pajarera
o junto a la encantada charla de alguna fuente.

A flor de tierra, amante. Casi sobre la tierra
donde el sol me caliente los huesos, y mis ojos,
alargados en tallos, suban a ver de nuevo
la lámpara salvaje de los ocasos rojos.

A flor de tierra, amante. Que el tránsito así sea
    más breve. Yo presiento
la lucha de mi carne por volver hacia arriba,
por sentir en sus átomos la frescura del viento.

Yo sé que acaso nunca allá abajo mis manos
    podrán estarse quietas.
Que siempre como topos arañarán la tierra
en medio de las sombras estrujadas y prietas.

Arrójame semillas. Yo quiero que se enraícen
en la greda amarilla de mis huesos menguados.
¡por la parda escalera de las raíces vivas
yo subiré a mirarte en los lirios morados!

Las Lenguas de Diamante

LIFE-HOOK

If I die, don't take me to the cemetery.
My grave is opening
right at the surface of the earth, near the laughing
clatter of some birdhouse,
near a fountain and its gossip.

Right at the surface, love. Almost above ground
where the sun can heat my bones, and my eyes
can climb the stems of plants to watch
the sunset, its fierce red lamp.

Right at the surface. So the passage
will be short. I already see
my body fighting to get back above the soil,
to feel the wind again.

I know my hands may never calm down.
The ghosts around me will be dim, juiceless, but my hands
will scratch like moles.

Sprout seeds for me. I want them growing
in the yellow chalk of my bones.
I'll climb the roots like a grey staircase, and watch you
from the purple lilies.

Translated by Marti Moody
Las Lenguas de Diamante

CRÓNICA

I

Todo lo que fué rosa eléctrica y heroica
en mí ya es sólo ahora dócil flor en sosiego,
no tienen las mañanas ni gamos ni juarías,
los ángeles no pasan sedientos por mi sueño.

Puedo abrirme las venas sin que la lenta sangre
se empoce entre la arcilla que marca mis pisadas
y sobre las rodillas he de mecer cien niños,
uno tras otro, quieta, sin emoción ni ansia.

II

Ya en mi garganta se ha cuajado el canto
desde que aquél se me durmió en la tierra.
Las cimbreantes abejas no persiguen
los huecos afiebrados de mis sienes
y estoy inmóvil, la mujer de acero,
junto al río sin juncos y sin peces.

Vienes tú ahora, hombre de ancha risa,
hombre de clavelinas y de tunas,
rico, vibrante, con los hombros fuertes
y ágiles remos en la mano enjuta.

Pasa no más. Mi oscura torrecilla
no ha de encender por nadie la lucerna
que la signaba azul: azul de versos
y de esperanza, cada día, nueva.
La mujer de metal rompió la lámpara
y entre las manos una adelfa lleva.

Perdida

48

CHRONICLE

I

Everything that was a rose, electric and heroic
is now only a docile flower at rest in me.
Mornings no longer signal packs of hounds or deer.
No thirsty angels pass through my sleep.

I can open my veins without the slow
trickle of my life's blood filling the clay where I step
and I will quietly rock a hundred children on my knee
one after another, no anxiety, no emotion.

II

My song is curdled in my throat
since the earth took him from me.
The vibrant bees stopped pursuing
the fevered hollows of my being
and I stand immobile, the woman of steel
by the river, no fish, no soft rushes.

You come now, wide smiling man,
song and flower man,
rich, vibrant, strong shouldered
agile oars in lean hands.

Go on by. My small dark tower
will not light for anyone
the blue light: blue verses,
blue hope, each day, new.
The metal woman broke the lamp.
In her hands she carries only
a laurel flower.

Translated by Nora Wieser
Perdida

Gabriela Mistral
Chile
1889–1957

GABRIELA MISTRAL (Lucila Godoy Alcayaga), the first Latin American to win the Nobel Prize for literature in 1945, was born in the Elqui Valley, a lush region in the north of Chile. Mistral was raised by her mother and an older sister after the father abandoned the family when Gabriela was barely three years old. These two women often sacrificed themselves to provide for Gabriela's education and upbringing. She was an unusually gifted child, sometimes ridiculed by her peers for her distracted day-dreaming. She trained as an elementary school teacher and quickly distinguished herself as an outstanding educator. In 1922 she was invited by the Mexican government to help establish educational reforms. This stay in Mexico began a series of visits to many countries. In the United States, for example, she taught at Barnard, Vassar and Middlebury. She had various diplomatic posts as a representative of Chile. From 1948 until her death, she had a residence in Santa Barbara, California. She died of cancer in the United States in 1957.

Her poetry has a predominant theme of love: a noble collective love of humanity in its universal dimensions, of children, of the countries and people she encounters; also Mistral is the personal expression of love which is often tragic because of the nature of her life experiences. She had a lover who committed suicide, she was rejected by another love, a young Chilean poet, and her adored nephew committed suicide in 1945 at the age of eighteen.

Her first book DESOLACIÓN, was published in 1922 in New York under the direction of the distinguished Hispanist, Federico de Onis, and a group of American professors who recognized the value of poems which until then had been scattered in various periodicals. The book included the Death Sonnets which had won Mistral a prize in Chile in 1914. These poems were written after the suicide of her lover.

Her third book TALA (Ruin) was written in 1938. The proceeds were donated to a Spanish children's Civil War refugee camp in France. It is a book which expressed Mistral's collective love for children, for the Hispanic peoples and her concern for social injustice. Her last book LAGAR (Wine Press) has an interesting section entitled "Locas Mujeres" (crazy women) with poems which include titles such as "La Desasida" (the detached woman), "La Desvelada" (the insomniac woman), "La Fugitiva" (the fugitive woman). These poems are the last in a part of Mistral's poetry which merits careful study. In her book TERNURA (Tenderness) 1925, she has a section entitled "La Desvariadora" (The Raving Woman). In TALA there is a section called "Historias de Loca" (Stories of a mad woman).

Books of Poetry

Desolación	1922
Ternura	1925
Tala	1938
Lagar	1954

LOS SONETOS DE LA MUERTE

I

Del nicho helado en que los hombres te pusieron,
te bajaré a la tierra humilde y soleada.
Que he de dormirme en ella los hombres no supieron,
y que hemos de soñar sobre la misma almohada.

Te acostaré en la tierra soleada con una
dulcedumbre de madre para el hijo dormido,
y la tierra ha de hacerse suavidades de cuna
al recibir tu cuerpo de niño dolorido.

Luego iré espolvoreando tierra y polvo de rosas,
y en la azulada y leve polvareda de luna,
los despojos livianos irán quedando presos.

Me alejaré cantando mis venganzas hermosas,
¡porque a ese hondor recóndito la mano de ninguna
bajará a disputarme tu puñado de huesos!

Desolación

DEATH SONNETS

I

I'll take you from the icy niche where they placed you,
lower you to the humble, sunny earth.
They didn't know that's where I'll die,
we'll sleep in the same bed.

Gently, a mother with her sleeping son,
I'll lay to bed in the earth.
It will be all softness for your body,
a cradle for a crying child.

Then I'll sprinkle rose-dust and earth,
and your spoils, almost weightless, will remain
imprisoned in the moon's blue cloud of dust.

I'll leave you, singing my beautiful revenge —
because no one's hand will drop to the secret depth
to contest your fistful of bones.

Translated by Marti Moody
Desolación

53

Este largo cansancio se hará mayor un día,
y el alma dirá al cuerpo que no quiere seguir
arrastrando su masa por la rosada vía,
por donde van los hombres, contentos de vivir . . .

Sentirás que a tu lado cavan briosamente,
que otra dormida llega a la quieta ciudad.
Esperaré que me hayan cubierto totalmente . . .
¡y después hablaremos por una eternidad!

Sólo entonces sabrás el por qué, no madura
para las hondas huesas tu carne todavía,
tuviste que bajar, sin fatiga, a dormir.

Se hará luz en la zona de los sinos, oscura;
sabrás que en nuestra alianza signo de astros había
y, roto el pacto enorme, tenías que morir . . .

Desolación

II

Someday when I'm even more tired
my soul will tell my body that it won't go on,
dragging its mass down the rosy way
with men who are content with life.

You'll feel them digging briskly at your side,
another sleeping person arrives in the quiet city.
I'll wait until they've covered me completely,
then we can talk forever!

Then you'll know why the flesh near your bones
doesn't age, why you descended
into sleep when you weren't tired.

The dark zones of the fates will be revealed.
You'll know our alliance was decreed by the stars,
and when our pact was broken, you had to die.

Translated by Marti Moody
Desolación

III

Malas manos tomaron tu vida desde el día
en que, a una señal de astros, dejara su plantel
nevado de azucenas. En gozo florecía.
Malas manos entraron trágicamente en él . . .

Y yo dije al Señor: "Por las sendas mortales
le llevan. ¡Sombra amada que no saben guiar!
¡Arráncalo, Señor, a esas manos fatales
o le hundes en el largo sueño que sabes dar!

¡No le puedo gritar, no le puedo seguir!
Su barca empuja un negro viento de tempestad.
Retórnalo a mis brazos o le siegas en flor."

Se detuvo la barca rosa de su vivir . . .
¿Que no sé del amor, que no tuve piedad?
¡Tú, que vas a juzgarme, lo comprendes, Señor!

Desolación

III

Evil hands took your life.
At a signal from the stars, it left
the nursery that was white with lilies.
It was happy growing there, but evil hands . . .

And I said to the Lord: "They're taking him by deadly paths.
They don't know how to guide
the spirit I love. Grab him from their hands
or sink him into your long sleep.

I can't shout to him, I can't
follow him! A black squall pushes his boat.
Bring him back to me, or cut him off in flower."

His life's rose boat was stopped.
—I don't know about love? I didn't have pity?
You who will judge me: you understand, Lord!

Translated by Marti Moody
Desolación

PAN

Dejaron un pan en la mesa,
mitad quemado, mitad blanco,
pellizcado encima y abierto
en unos migajones de ampo.

Me parece nuevo o como no visto,
y otra cosa que él no me ha alimentado,
pero volteando su miga, sonámbula,
tacto y olor se me olvidaron.

Huele a mi madre cuando dio su leche,
huele a tres valles por donde he pasado:
a Aconcagua, a Pátzcuaro, a Elqui,
y a mis entrañas cuando yo canto.

Otros olores no hay en la estancia
y por eso él así me ha llamado;
y no hay nadie tampoco en la casa
sino este pan abierto en un plato,
que con su cuerpo me reconoce
y con el mío yo reconozco.

Se ha comido en todos los climas
el mismo pan en cien hermanos:
pan de Coquimbo, pan de Oaxaca,
pan de Santa Ana y de Santiago.

En mis infancias yo le sabía
forma de sol, de pez o de halo,
y sabía mi mano su miga
y el calor de pichón emplumado . . .

Después le olvidé hasta este día
en que los dos nos encontramos,
yo con mi cuerpo de Sara vieja
y él con el suyo de cinco años.

BREAD

They've left a loaf of bread
out on the table — half-burnt, half-white,
pinched on top and open,
a few snowy crumbs.

It looks fresh, as if
no one had looked at it yet,
and only bread has nourished me.
But turning a piece in my fingers, I drift off,
forget how it feels and smells.

And I can smell my mother's milk,
Aconcagua, Pátzcuaro, Elqui,
the three valleys I've passed through,
and my insides when I sing.

Other odors aren't in the room,
it's the bread that calls me.
No one in the house
except for this loaf on a plate
that knows me with its body
as I know it with mine.

In every land they eat this,
the same bread in a hundred brothers
Coquimbo bread, Oaxaca bread,
the bread of Santiago, Santa Ana.

As a child I knew it
shaped like a sun, fish, or halo;
my hands knew its crumbs,
warm as a young pigeon.

Then I forgot it, until today
we found ourselves together,
my body old as Sarah's
next to a five-year-old child.

Amigos muertos con que comíalo
en otros valles sientan el vaho
de un pan en septiembre molido
y en agosto en Castilla segado.

Es otro y es el que comimos
en tierras donde se acostaron.
Abro la miga y les doy su calor;
lo volteo y les pongo su hálito.

La mano tengo de él rebosada
y la mirada puesta en mi mano;
entrego un llanto arrepentido
por el olvido de tantos años,
y la cara se me envejece
y me renace en este hallazgo.

Como se halla vacía la casa,
estemos juntos los reencontrados,
sobre esta mesa sin carne y fruta,
los dos en este silencio humano,
hasta que seamos otra vez uno
y nuestro día haya acabado . . .

Tala

60

Dead friends I've eaten with
in other valleys: feel the mist
of a bread ground in September,
reaped in the August of Castille.

It's a different bread, and the same
we ate together, in the lands
where they lay down to die.
I break the piece, give them its warmth
turn it in my fingers,
offer them a breath.

My hand is filled with bread,
my gaze is on my hand.
I break into tears, sorry
for forgetting whole years, and my face
grows old on me, or is reborn
in this discovery.

Since the house is empty.
Let us, the reencountered, be together
at this table without meat or fruit,
the two of us
in a human silence,
until our day has ended
and we're one again.

Translated by Marti Moody
Tala

Claudia Lars
El Salvador
1899-1974

THERE ARE AT LEAST two women among the 20th century poets in Latin America who seem to epitomize the ideal of the maternal woman. Since motherhood is a sacrosanct institution in the Latin American society, these two women have a devoted following. One of these women is Gabriela Mistral. The other is Claudia Lars. Both women were beloved for their generosity and compassion.

Claudia Lars, as yet, is not as well known as Gabriela Mistral, but her poetry has the same intensity of feeling. There is always a ring of authenticity in her poems; the reader never doubts the feelings as being genuine, regardless of the variance in the quality of expression. One comes away from reading Claudia Lars with an overriding sense of honesty. In addition, the tone has a fragility that makes the images seem to be woven in whispers. In a brief poem from a series entitled *Migajas* (Crumbs) she tells us about her view of poetry:

> Each revelation of poetry
> ought to be a very intimate secret.
> Sometimes I am sobered by the sin
> of trying to give away the ineffable,
> then I envy a man who plants a tree
> in silent humility.

Perhaps among the best examples of the authenticity and the delicate tones are the fifteen poems entitled "Cartas Escritas Cuando Crece la Noche" (Letters Written When Night Grows). David Escobar Galindo, a fellow poet, explains the circumstances of these poems.[1] It seems they are the reply to three sonnets she received after forty years of silence, from a poet out of the country. This relationship had been the inspiration for some of the poems in her first book published in 1934, ESTRELLAS EN EL POZO. (Stars in the Hole).

Claudia Lars' "letters" of reply were written in August of 1972. She sent them to David Escobar Galindo with the following note:

My very dear friend,

I place in your hands this series of letters - poems, unedited and coming from my heart. The person I sent them to, hasn't yet told me if he received them. Hopefully they haven't been lost in the mail.

I leave Thursday the 28th for New Orleans. I have a serious illness. I'm not depressed, since death is for me the Great Sleep of a While or the Other Face of Life. I hope I can see you again. In this world (when I take account of what I've lived) I've been very happy.

Claudia Lars

who loves you and admires you.

(She went to New Orleans to seek medical treatment for the cancer that caused her death two years later). Upon her death, the mysterious poet published a series of poems dedicated to Claudia Lars under the pseudonym of Juan d'Astil.[2]

Books of Poetry

Estrellas en el Pozo	1934
La Casa de Vidrio	1942
Ciudad Bajo mi Voz	1946
Sonetos	1947
La Canción Redonda	1947
Donde Llegan los Pasos	1955
Escuela de Pájaros	1955
Romances de Norte y Sur	1956
Tierra de Infancia	1958
Fábula de una Verdad	1959
Nuestro Pulsante Mundo	1959
Sobre el Ángel y el Hombre	1962
Del Fino Amanacer	1967
Apuntes. Obra Inédita. Cartas Escritas Cuando Crece la Noche. *Póstuma.*	1975

1. The explanation is found in the edition of Claudia Lars' last poems *Poesía Última* 1970–73) published by the Ministry of Education in San Salvador, 1975.

2. These poems are found in the magazine *Caracol*, no. 2, 1976. The magazine is an organ of the cultural promotion department of the National University of San Salvador.

CARTAS ESCRITAS CUANDO CRECE LA NOCHE
(Agosto de 1972)

I

El tiempo regresó -en un instante-
a la casa donde mi juventud
quiso comerse el cielo.

Lo demás bien lo sabes . . .

Otros llegaron con sus palabras
y sus cuerpos,
buscándome dolorosamente
o dejando la niebla del camino
entre mis pobres manos.

Lo demás es silencio . . .

Hoy tengo tus poemas en mis lágrimas
y el deseado mensaje -tan tuyo-
entra en mi corazón con mil años de ausencia.

Poesía Última

LETTERS WRITTEN WHEN NIGHT GROWS

(August 1972)

I

Time returned -in an instant-
to the house where my youth
wanted to devour the sky.

The rest you know well . . .

Others arrived with their words
and their bodies
painfully searching for me
or leaving the fog from the road
in my enfeebled hands.

The rest is silence . . .

Today I have your poems in my tears
and the message, -so yours-
penetrates me with the absence of a thousand years.

What's left is to possess this miracle
and feel myself as a new rose
at the edges of the Great Sleep.
Take my hand, finally and forever.

Translated by Leslie Keffer
Poesía Última

III

Pude haber vivido cerca de ti
suavemente
y encender tu lámpara y sentarme
en el ancho sillón oloroso a tiempo.

Pude cortar una rosa
y ponerla en tu escritorio
o bordar a media tarde
un enjardinado mantel.

Ocurrió lo contrario:
lejos anduve y sola
-tremendamente sola-
porque no quisiste acompañarme.
Pero en idas y venidas por esos caminos,
¡qué bien me enseñaron a conocer
quién soy!

Poesía Última

III

I could have lived close to you
gently
lit your lamp sitting
in the big chair scented with time.

I would have been able to cut a rose
and place it on your desk
or in late afternoon embroider
the trim on a table cloth.

The opposite happened:
I walked vast distances alone
-tremendously alone-
you didn't want to accompany me.
But coming and going on those roads,
how well they taught me to know
who I am!

Translated by Leslie Keffer
Poesía Última

VI

Si todo fuera distinto
yo no tendría un largo viaje en los ojos
y en esta soledad
versos y versos . . .

Si todo fuera distinto
yo sería a tu lado una dicha completa
y la mitad de tu alma.

Poesía Última

VI

If everything were different
I would not have a long journey
and solitude with
verses and verses . . .

If everything were different
I would be by your side as a completed saying
and a half of your soul.

Translated by Leslie Keffer
Poesía Última

VIII

El tiempo . . . ¿Qué es el tiempo? . . .
Para mí no ha pasado
desde aquellas noches de lunas amarillas,
cuando me llevabas a las reuniones de los sábados . . .

Me sentí joven al leer tus poemas
y me dio vergüenza experimentar esa dicha.
Con un gajo de sueños juveniles
Caí en profundo sueño.

Hoy me burlo del tiempo y hasta le hago cosquillas
en las barbas.
Así, medio jugando,
voy a meterlo por un mes
en el armario.

Poesía Última

VIII

Time . . . What is time?
for me it hasn't passed
since those nights, moon yellow
when you took me to Saturday parties . . .

I felt young reading your poems
and I was embarrassed feeling so.
Clutching adolescent dreams close,
I slept soundly.

Today I make fun of time, even tickling him
in his beard.
So, half playing
I'll put him in the closet
for a month.

Translated by Leslie Keffer
Poesía Última

X

Hay muchos años entre mi amor
y tu ausencia.
Con ellos puedo escribir
una historia larga.

Hay mil cosas que quisiera decirte
dulcemente . . .
¿Pero cómo expresar lo inefable?

Poesía Última

X

So many years between my love
and your absence.
With all these I could write
a long history.

There are a thousand things I would like to tell you
softly . . .
But how does one express the ineffable?

Translated by Leslie Keffer
Poesía Última

XI

Tal vez nunca contestes mis cartas.
Ya nada espero ni pido nada.

A estas horas sería ridículo preguntar al cartero
si me trae un sobre que brilla
como un pequeño astro.

Poesía Última

XI

Perhaps you will never answer my letters.
At this age I don't hope or ask for anything.

Wouldn't it be absurd to ask the mailman
if he's bringing a letter that shines
like a tiny star?

Translated by Leslie Keffer
Poesía Última

XIV

Cuando todo se cumpla
-en otra vida, porque aquí ya es muy tarde-
conoceré mejor el poder de los recuerdos
y viviré en tu casa.

Poesía Última

XIV

When all is fulfilled
in another life, because it's too late here—
I will know better the power of memories
and I will live in your house.

Translated by Leslie Keffer
Poesía Última

XV

Y ahora un "hasta siempre" . . . un "te agradezco" . . .
Descubrí mi esperanza.
Aquí se anuncia la mañana con un ángel
y con una semillita de antigüedad.

Poesía Última

XV

And now a "goodbye forever" . . . a "thank you" . . .
I have discovered my hope.
Here, morning is announced by an angel
and a small seed of antiquity.

Translated by Leslie Keffer
Poesía Última

EVOCACIÓN DE GABRIELA MISTRAL

Tu retiro apenas recogía
rumores de la ciudad mecanizada:
isla para viajeros locos,
llena de ciruelas y libros.

No olvido nuestras lecturas
bajo una lámpara,
ni las visitas del escritor noruego
que hablaba de la cuarta dimensión
como si hablara de Oslo.
Fácilmente regreso a los álamos azules
y a ciertos afanes mañaneros
entre remolachas y coles.

Mariposas sin rumbo
querían descansar en tu cabeza
y el perro destructor de escarabajos
se transformaba al oír nuestras voces
en cordero de Felpa.

Un Buda de marfil tenía asiento
cerca del libro más cristiano entre todos
y el Cristo medioeval en su cruz de viernes
agonizaba encima de la consola.

Tu profunda mirada
iba del Tranquilo Compasivo al Amoroso Sufriente
afirmando que los dos podían alumbrar la tierra entera
desde un mismo candelabro.

Casa tan quieta y limpia
me obligaba a caminar de puntillas
y era dulce recibir, sin pedirlo,
el oro de tu palabra.

EVOCATION OF GABRIELA MISTRAL

Your hideaway barely picked up
rumors of the mechanized city:
island for insane travelers,
full of books and plums

> I don't forget our readings
> under the lamp,
> nor the Norwegian writer's visits
> who spoke of the fourth dimension
> as if he spoke of Oslo.
> I'm easily returned to the blue poplars
> and certain morning chores
> among the beets and cabbage

Butterflies with no direction
wanted to rest on your head
and the dog, destroyer of beetles,
on hearing your voice, turned
into a docile lamb.

> A marble Buddha had a seat
> near the most Christian book of all
> and the medieval Christ on his Friday cross
> agonized on top of the console.

Your profound gaze
went from the tranquil compassionate one to the loving martyr
affirming that both could light the whole earth
from the same source.

> Such a clean quiet house
> made me walk on tiptoes
> and I received your words of
> gold, gently, without asking.

Gocé un verano inmerecido
y rompí noches del corazón
queriendo descubrir abismos.
Por eso al fin dijiste con voz resignada:
"Amiga curiosísima:
llegas hasta mis huesos para observarme
y ya ves: me han matado mis muertos" . . .

Entonces comprendí las líneas
de un rostro severo
y ahora padezco el largo fuego
en todos tus versos.

(En su casa de Santa Barbara, California)

I enjoyed an undeserved summer
and I burst through the soul's nights
wanting to discover chasms.
That's why you finally said with resignation:
"Most curious friend:
You have arrived at my very bones to observe me
and you see now: my own dead have killed me."

  Then I understood the lines
  of an austere face
  and now I suffer the fire
  of all your poems.

(At her house in Santa Barbara, California)
Translated by Nora Wieser

Cecilia Meireles

Brazil

1901–1964

IN BRAZIL, Cecilia Meireles achieved a distinguished reputation. She was awarded posthumously, the Premio Machado de Assis in 1965 for her complete works. She corroborated in most of the literary journals of note in Brazil, contributing scholarly criticism as well as poetry. She also helped found the first children's library in Brazil. In addition, because of her deep interest in folklore, she was elected secretary of the First National Folklore Congress. As a representative of Brazil she traveled widely, lecturing in countries such as the United States, Portugal, Mexico and Uruguay. One of her books of poetry is inspired by a visit to India. (POEMAS ESCRITAS NA INDIA).

She published her first book of poetry in 1919. Often her poems are long and deceptively simple. She avoided the social themes of the war years and was sometimes criticised for her aloofness. It is only recently that the significance of her work comes to light as it becomes the subject of careful critical analysis.

The long poem "Mar Absoluto" is from her book of the same title which appeared in 1945. The majesty of this poem seems to ensure its place among the best poems of the sea tradition. Especially noteworthy is the tremendously vibrant, cyclic and regenerative force that the sea has in the poem by Meireles.

Books of Poetry

Viagem	1939
Vaga Música	1942
Mar Absoluto e Outros Poemas	1945
Retrato Natural	1949
Amor en Leonoreta	1951
Doze Noturnos da Holanda e Oaeronauta	1952
Romanceiro da Inconfidencia	1953
Poemas Escritas na India	
Pequeño Oratorio de Santa Clara	1955
Pistoia, Cemeterio Militar Brasileiro	1955
Cancoes	1956
Romance de Santa Cecilia	1957
Cu Isto ou Aquilo	1965
Cronica Trovada	1965
Metal Rosicler	1960
Solombra	1963

MAR ABSOLUTO

Foi desde sempre o mar.
E multidões passadas me empurravam
como o barco esquecido.

Agora recordo que falavam
da revolta dos ventos,
de linhos, de cordas, de ferros,
de sereias dadas à costa.

E o rosto de meus avós estava caido
pelos mares do Oriente, com seus corais e pérolas,
e pelos mares do Norte, duros de gelo.

Então, é comigo que falam,
sou eu que devo ir.
Porque não há mais ninguém
não, não haverá mais ninguém,
tão decidido a amar e a obedecer a seus mortos.

E tenho de procurar meus tios remotos afogados.
Tenho de levar-lhes redes de rezas,
campos convertidos em velas,
barcas sobrenaturais
com peixes mensageiros
e santos náuticos.

E fico tonta,
acordada de repente nas prais tumultuosas.
E apressama-me, e não me deixam sequer mirar a rosa-dos-ventos.

"Para adiante! Pelo mar largo!
Livrando o corpo da lição frágil da areia!

Ao mar! — Disciplina humana para a empresa da vida!"

Meu sangue entende-se com essas vozes poderosas.
A solidez da terra, monótona,
parece-nos fraca ilusão.

ABSOLUTE SEA

The sea was and is forever.
And multitudes from the past propelled me
like an abandoned boat.

I recall now they were speaking
of wind revolts,
of linens, ropes and ironware,
of mermaids marooned on the coast.

And the face of my forefathers was turned
by the coral and pearl seas of the Orient
and ice hard seas of the North.

Now, the multitudes speak with me
it is I who must go.
Because there is no one,
no, nor will there ever be anyone
so determined to love and obey his dead.

And I must search for my remote, drowned uncles.
I must carry them nets of prayer,
fields converted to sails,
supernatural ships,
with messenger fish
and nautical saints.

And I am dazed,
suddenly awakened on tumultuous shores.
My ancestors hurry me, not permitting a look at the compass.

"Onward! Through the open sea!
Freeing the body from the fragile lesson of sand!
Seaward! —Human discipline for life's enterprise."

My blood agrees with those powerful voices.
the monotonous solidity of land
seems a weak illusion.

Queremos a ilusão grande do mar,
multiplicada em suas malhas de perigo.

Queremos a sua solidão robusta,
uma solidão para todos os lados,
uma ausência humana que se opõe ao mesquinho formigar do
      mundo,
e faz o tempo inteiriço, livre das lutas de cada dia.

O alento heróico do mar tem sue pólo secreto,
que os homens sentem, seduzidos e medrosos.

O mar é só mar, desprovido de apegos,
matando-se e recuperando-se,
correndo como um touro azul por sua própria sombra,
e arremetendo com bravura contra ninguém,
e sendo depois a pura sombra de si mesmo,
por si mesmo vencido. É o seu grande exercício.

Não precisa do destino fixo da terra,
ele que, ao mesmo tempo,
é o dançarino e a sua dança.

Tem um reino de metamorfose, para experiência:
seu corpo é o seu próprio jogo,
e a sua eternidade lúdica
não apenas gratuita; más perfeita.

Baralha seus altos contrastes:
cavalo epico, anêmona suave,
entrega-se todo, despreza tudo,
sustenta no seu prodigioso rítimo
jardins, estrelas, cuadas, antenas, olhos,
mas é desfolhado, cego, nu, dono apenas de si,
da sua terminante grandeza despojada.

Não se esquece que é água, ao desdobrar suas visões:
água de todas as possibilidades,
más sem fraqueza nenhuma.

We want the immense illusion of the sea,
multiplied by its mails of danger.

We want its robust aloneness,
a solitude on all sides,
a human absence opposed to petty ant-like actions of the world;
that renders time whole, free from daily exertions.

The sea's heroic breath has its secret pole,
which men sense, seduced, stricken.

The sea is only sea, no ties,
killing itself and recuperating,
running like a blue bull through its own shadow,
charging fiercely against no one,
and afterwards being its own pure shadow
by its own self conquered. This is its great exercise.

The sea has no need for the fixed destiny of land,
being at the same time,
the dancer and the dance.

For experience, it has a realm of metamorphosis,
its body is its own game,
and playful eternity
not only free: but perfect.

The sea jumbles its soaring contrasts:
epic steed, soft anemone,
delivering itself totally, scorning everything,
sustaining in the prodigious rhythm
gardens, stars, tails, antennas, eyes,
but it is leafless, blind, naked, master only of itself,
of the final spoils of grandeur.

Unfolding visions, the sea does not forget that it is water,
of many possibilities
but without weakness.

E assim como água fala-me.
Atira-me búzios, como lembranca de sua voz,
e estrelas eriçadas, como convite ao meu destino.

Não me chama para que siga por cima dele,
nem por dentro de si:
mas para que me converta nele mesmo. É o seu máximo dom.

Não me quer arrastar como meus tios outrora,
nem lentamente conduzida,
como meus avós, de serenos alhos certeiros.

Aceita-me apenas convertida em sua natureza:
plástica, fluida, disponível,
igual a ele, em constante solilóquio,
sem exigências de princípio e fim,
desprendida de terra e céu.

E eu, que viera cautelosa,
por procurar gente passada,
suspeito que me enganei,
que há outras ordens que não foram bem ouvidas;
que uma outra boca falava: não sòmente a de antigos mortos,
e o mar a que me mandam não é apenas este mar.

Não é apenas este mar que reboa nas minhas vidraças,
mas outro, que se parece com ele
como se parecem os vultos dos sonhos dormidos.
E entre água e estrela estudo a solidão.

E recordo minha herança de cordas e âncoras,
e encontro tudo sobre-humano.
E este mar visível levanta para mim
uma face espantosa.

And so as water it speaks to me.
Throwing me shells as a reminder of its voice,
and bristly stars as an invitation to my destiny.

The sea does not call me to follow on top
or within
but to convert my being into itself.
That is its greatest talent.

Nor does the sea wish
to drag me as my uncles long ago,
or lead me slowly
like my forefathers, they of serene, unerring eyes.

It accepts me only transformed into itself:
plastic, fluid, accessible,
equal, in a constant soliloquy,
with no requests from beginning to end,
detached from sea and land.

And I who came cautiously,
searching for ancestors,
sense that I deceived myself,
there are other orders, not heard:
another voice speaking: not only that of the ancient dead,
and the sea where they send me is not only this sea.

It is not only this sea that resounds on my window
but another, a resemblance
as dream shapes resemble one another.
And between the water and a star I study the solitude.

I recall my inheritance of ropes and anchors,
and find everything superhuman.
And this visible sea lifts up before me
a terrifying face.

E retrai-se, ao dizer o que preciso.
E é logo uma pequena concha fervilhante,
nódua líquida e instável,
célula azul sumindo-se
no reino de um outro mar:
ah! do Mar Absoluto.

Mar Absoluto

Withdrawing, telling me what I need.
And soon becoming a small seething shell.
liquid and unstable spot,
a blue cell disappearing
into the realm of another sea:
Ah! the Absolute Sea.

Translated by Darlene J. Sadlier
Mar Absoluto

Olga Orozco
Argentina

IF YOU SHOULD MEET Olga Orozco in Buenos Aires, you will not easily forget her. She is fascinating. But the fascination is not due to what she says because she is apt to say very little. Physically she is dark skinned, black haired, fiftyish. It is her eyes. They are an intensely vivid green-blue color. Even more important, there is something ageless about them — almost as if they had been passed down through time — as if Olga Orozco were only their temporary guardian. Someone once called her "the magician of memory." You feel something of the "maga" in her, as she looks intently at you across her living room. On the wall are hung African ritual masks from her travels. The masks themselves seem to pulsate as she speaks calmly in a low, throaty voice . . . it is only the gaze that is profound and mysterious. She talks about astrology. (She is a confirmed believer). She jokes about the ridiculous censorship in her country. She also laughs — the wonderfully healthy laugh of a person who has learned its value as an alternative to despair.

All of Olga Orozco is in her poetry. She is prone to conjure other worlds, other kinds of spaces which her protagonists enter and explore. Often these protagonists are parts of a fragmented self. The verbal creativity in Orozco is parallel to the visual creativity of the surrealist painter: depicting the objects that surround us in new, hitherto unexplored dimensions which result in a heightened awareness of their existence.

The rigidity implied in labels makes one hesitate to call all of her work surrealist. She has collaborated with a certain movement of surrealism in Argentina; for example, contributing poems to a short lived literary magazine called A PARTIR DE CERO (Starting from Zero) in the mid 1950's. The magazine also published texts from the French surrealists Artaud, Eluard, Péret and Breton. Her most recent book MUSEO SALVAJE 1974 (The Savage Museum) is an exploration of the parts of the human body, the mouth, the eyes, the blood, the skin, for example. She describes regions and functions of these body parts with fresh, vibrant images which stem from an imaginative unconstricted contemplation of their reality. If someone insists, the book could be placed within the confines of surrealism.

To do the same with LAS MUERTES 1952 (The Deaths) is more difficult. The book is a series of poems about the deaths of fictional characters. There are poems to Melville's Bartleby, to the Prodigal Son, to Evangeline, to Lautréamont's Maldorar, to Rilke's Christoph Detlev Brigge, among others. In the introductory poem, she says:

Here are some dead whose bones won't make the rain white . . .
They are the dead with no flowers . . .
. . . their deaths are the exasperated faces of our life.

The last poem in the book is entitled "Olga Orozco."

Books of Poetry

Desde Lejos	1946
La Muertes	1952
Los Juegos Peligrosos	1962
Museo Salvaje	1974

"OLGA OROZCO"

Yo, Olga Orozco, desde tu corazón digo a todos que muero.
Amé la soledad, la heroica perduración de toda fe,
el ocio donde crecen animales extraños y plantas fabulosas,
la sombra de un gran tiempo que pasó entre misterios y entre
    alucinaciones,
y también el pequeño temblor de las bujías en el anochecer.
Mi historia está en mis manos y en las manos con que otros las
    tatuaron.
De mi estadía quedan las magias y los ritos,
unas fechas gastadas por el soplo de un despiadado amor,
la humareda distante de la casa donde nunca estuvimos,
y unos gestos dispersos entre los gestos de otros que no me
    conocieron.
Lo demás aún se cumple en el olvido,
aún labra la desdicha en el rostro de aquella que se buscaba en
    mí igual que en un espejo de sonrientes praderas,
y a la que tú verás extrañamente ajena:
mi propia aparecida condenada a mi forma de este mundo.
Ella hubiera querido guardarme en el desdén o en el orgullo,
en el último instante fulmíneo como el rayo,
no en el túmulo incierto donde alzo todavía la voz ronca y llorada
entre los remolinos de tu corazón.
No. Esta muerte no tiene descanso ni grandeza.
No puedo estar mirándola por primera vez durante tanto tiempo.
Pero debo seguir muriendo hasta tu muerte
porque soy tu testigo ante una ley más honda y más oscura que
    los cambiantes sueños,
allá, donde escribimos la sentencia:
"Ellos han muerto ya.
Se habían elegido por castigo y perdón, por cielo y por infierno.
Son ahora una mancha de humedad en las paredes del primer
    aposento."

Las Muertes

96

"OLGA OROZCO"

I, Olga Orozco, tell everyone from your heart that I die.
I loved solitude, the heroic duration of all faith,
idleness where strange animals and fabulous plants grow,
the shadow of a great time that passed between mysteries and
    hallucinations,
and also the slight tremble of candles in the nightfall.
My history lies in my hands and in the hands of others who
    tatooed them.
Rites, magic, dates worn by the breath of a merciless love,
remain from my sojourn,
clouds of distant smoke belonging to the house where we never
    were,
and some gestures scattered among those of people who never
    knew me.
The rest is fulfilled in oblivion,
misfortune is still in the face of one who searched for herself in me
    as in a mirror of smiling meadowlands,
and you shall see her strangely foreign:
my own likeness condemned to my form in this world,
wishing to keep me, in scorn or pride
in the last thunderous instant, as a flash of lightning
and not in the uncertain disorder, among the whirlpools of the
    soul, where I still lift my hoarse and mournful voice.
No. This death has no rest or grandeur.
I'm not able to look at it for long, the first time.
But it seems I'll continue dying until your death
because I am your witness before a law deeper and darker than
    changing dreams,
"They have already died.
They were chosen for penalty and pardon, for heaven and hell.
They are now a stain caused by humidity on the walls of the first
    chamber."

Translated by Leslie Keffer
Las Muertes

97

NOICA
(Personaje de un cuadro de J. Batlle Planas)

Nunca oísteis su nombre.
Sin embargo, cuando un sueño cualquiera entretejió fosforescentes
    redes sobre el rostro del tiempo,
Noica estuvo.
Tal vez su cabellera fuera para vosotros la marea letárgica por
    donde sube al cielo la primer Navidad
-esa novia que flota con su ramo de cristal escarchado y una cinta
    plateada en la garganta-.
Acaso sus ropajes fueran para vosotros un ámbito en que caen
    lentamente las hojas,
cuando el amor golpea con sus manos el follaje encantado.
Lo cierto es que fue Noica,
la diosa de los seres subterráneos que disponen callando el
    esplendor del mundo.
Reconocedla ahora.
Antes que se haya ido para ser melodía de polvo contra el vidrio,
    sombra musgosa de los muros.
Guardadla para siempre en esta misma puerta abierta en el celaje
    de los siglos,
donde se balancea, despidiéndose,
como la luminaria en el claro final de la arboleda.
Del otro lado yace su reino alucinado.
Nunca entraréis en él.
Juntos se abismarán debajo del recuerdo y del olvido.

Las Muertes

NOICA
(A character in a painting by J. Batlle Planas)

You never heard her name.
Nevertheless, when any dream interwove phosphorescent
 nets over the face of time,
Noica was there.
Perhaps for you, her hair was the lethargic tide on which the
 first Christmas rose to heaven
-this maiden who floats with her bough of frosted crystal and a
 silver ribbon on her throat-.
Perhaps for you, her garments are a niche for gentle falling leaves,
when love strikes the enchanted foliage with her hands.
It had to be Noica,
the goddess of subterranean beings that quietly arrange
 the splendour of the world.
Recognize her now.
Before she leaves to become a melody of dust against the glass, a
 mossy shadow on the walls.
Guard her forever in this same open door among the clouds of
 centuries,
where she balances, taking her leave,
as the light at the clear edge of the wooded grove.
On the other side is her hallucinated kingdom.
You shall never enter it.
Together they shall descend to the depths of memories and
 oblivion.

Translated by Leslie Keffer
Las Muertes

LAMENTO DE JONÁS

Este cuerpo tan denso con que clausuro todas las salidas,
este saco de sombras cosido a mis dos alas
no me impide pasar hasta el fondo de mí:
una noche cerrada donde vienen a dar todos los espejismos de la
  noche,
unas aguas absortas donde moja sus pies la esfinge de otro mundo.

Aquí suelo encontrar vestigios de otra edad,
fragmentos de panteones no disueltos por la sal de mi sangre,
oráculos y faunas aspirados por las cenizas de mi porvenir.
A veces aparecen continentes en vuelo, plumas de otros ropajes
  sumergidos;
a veces permanecen casi como el anuncio de la resurrección.

Pero es mejor no estar.
Porque hay trampas aquí.
Alguien juega a no estar cuando yo estoy
o me observa conmigo desde las madrigueras de cada soledad.
Alguien simula un foso entre el sueño y la piel para que me deslice
  hasta el último abismo de los otros
o me induce a escarbar debajo de mi sombra.

Es difícil salir.
Me tapian con un muro que solamente corre hacia nunca jamás;
me eligen para morir la duración;
me anudan a las venas de un organismo ciego que me exhala y me
  aspira sin cesar.

Y el corazón, en tanto,
¿en dónde el corazón,
el tambor de nostalgias que convoca en tinieblas a todos los
  relevos?
Por no hablar de este cuerpo,
de este guardián opaco que me transporta y me retiene
y me arroja consigo en una náusea desde los pies a la cabeza.

JONAH'S LAMENT

This dense body with which I close all exists,
this sack of shadows sewed to my two wings
doesn't stop me from entering my own depths:
a closed night where all the night's mirages come to rest,
waters where another world's sphinx wets her feet.
Here I tend to find traces of another time,
graveyard fragments not dissolved by salt from my blood,
oracles and fauns inhaled by the ashes of my future.
Continents in flight sometimes appear, feathers of other submerged
    garments;
and other times they persist almost like the omen of the resurrection.

But it's better not to be here.
Because there are traps.
Someone plays at not being here when I am
or observes me with myself from the haunts of every solitude.
Someone simulates a depth between the illusion and my skin so that
    I may slip to the last abyss of the others
or induce myself to dig beneath my shadow.

It's difficult to leave.
They surround me with a wall that only goes toward "never";
they elect me to die for the duration;
they tie me to the veins of a blind being that exhales and inhales
    me unceasingly.

And meanwhile the heart,
where is the heart,
the drum of nostalgia which convokes all reliefs in darkness?
I don't talk about this body,
this opaque guardian that transports me and retains me
and hurls me with him in a nausea from head to foot.

Soy mi propio rehén,
el pausado veneno del verdugo,
el pacto con la muerte.
¡Y quién ha dicho acaso que este fuera un lugar para mí?

Museo Salvaje

I am my own hostage
the slow poison of an executioner
the agreement with death.

And who, by chance, has said that this was a place for me?

Translated by Leslie Keffer
Museo Salvaje

ESFINGES SUELEN SER

Una mano, dos manos. Nada más.
Todavía me duelen las manos que me faltan,
esas que se quedaron adheridas a la barca fantasma que me trajo
y sacuden la costa con golpes de tambor,
con puñados de arena contra el agua de migraciones y nostalgias.
Son manos transparentes que deslizan el mundo debajo de mis pies,
que vienen y se van.
Pero estas que prolongan mi espesa anatomía
más allá de cualquier posible hoguera,
un poco más acá de cualquier imposible paraíso,
no son manos que sirvan para entreabrir las sombras,
para quitar los velos y volver a cerrar.
Yo no entiendo estas manos.
Sí, demasiado próximas,
demasiado distantes,
ajenas como mi propio vuelo acorralado adentro de otra piel,
como el insomnio de alguien que huye inalcanzable por mis dedos.
A veces las encuentro casi a punto de ocultarme de mí
o de apostar el resto en favor de otro cuerpo,
de otro falso plumaje que conspira con la noche y el sol.
Me inquietan estas manos que juegan al misterio y al azar.
Cambian mis alimentos por regueros de hormigas,
buscan una sortija en el desierto,
transforman la inocencia en un cuchillo,
perseveran absortas como valvas en la malicia y el error.
Cuando las miro pliegan y despliegan abanicos furtivos,
una visión errante que se pierde entre plumas, entre alas de saqueo,
mientras ellas se siguen, se persiguen,
crecen hasta cubrir la inmensidad o reducen a polvo el cuenco de
    mis días.

SPHINXES INCLINED TO BE

One hand, two hands. Nothing more.
I still hurt from the hands I lack,
those that remained glued to the fantasmal boat that brought me
and shake the coast with drum rolls
and fistfuls of sand against nostalgic, migrant waters.
Transparent hands that make the world slip beneath my feet,
that come to me and go away again.
But these hands that extend my dense body
beyond any possible hearth
further than any impossible paradise,
they are not hands which open the shadows ever so slightly,
to remove the veils, bolting them shut once again.
I don't understand these hands.
Yes, much too near,
and yet too distant,
foreign as my own flight corraled inside another's skin,
as the insomnia of one who flees beyond reach of my fingers.
Sometimes I find them almost hiding myself from me
or betting in favor of another ornamented body
that conspires with night and sun.
They make me uneasy, these hands which play with mystery and
    chance.
They change my food for streams of ants,
they search for a ring in the desert,
they transform the innocent into knives,
persevering as valves in malice and error.
When I watch them they pleat and unpleat evasive fans,
a wandering vision which loses itself between feathers and wings of
    plunder,
while they follow themselves, pursue themselves,
these hands grow till they cover immensity or reduce to dust my
    hollow days.

Son como dos esfinges que tejen mi condena con la mitad del
    crimen,
con la mitad de la misericordia.
Y esa expresión de peces atrapados,
de pájaros ansiosos,
de impasibles harpías con que asisten a su propio ritual!
Esta es la ceremonia del contagio y la peste hasta la idolatría.
Una caricia basta para multiplicar esas semillas negras que
    propagan la lepra,
esas fosforescencias que propagan la seda y el ardor,
esos hilos errantes que propagan el naufragio y la sed.
¡Y esa brasa incesante que deslizan de la una a la otra
como un secreto al rojo,
como una llama que quema demasiado!
Me pregunto, me digo
qué trampa están urdiendo desde mi porvenir estas dos manos.
Y sin embargo son las mismas manos.
Nada más que dos manos extrañamente iguales a dos manos en su
    oficio de manos,
desde el principio hasta el final.

Museo Salvaje

They are as two sphinxes that weave my condemnation
into a half of crime,
and a half of mercy.
And this expression of trapped fish,
anxious birds,
impassive vulture men who assist at their own ritual!
a wicked, contagious ceremony, idolatrous plague.
One caress is enough to multiply black seeds of leprosy,
and phosphorous beams which propagate silk and passion,
errant threads that weave calamity and thirst.
And that incessant ember that slips from one to the other
as a reddened secret,
as a flame which burns far too much!
I ask myself, I tell myself
what trap from future time are these two hands plotting
yet they are the same hands.
Nothing more than two hands, strangely alike, two hands in their
    duty of being just hands.
from beginning to end.

Translated by Leslie Keffer
Museo Salvaje

The Nicaraguan Group

Mariana Sanson	1918
Lygia Guillén	1939
Vidaluz Meneses	1944
Ana Ilce	1945
Gioconda Belli	1947
Rosario Murillo	1951
Yolanda Blanco	1954

IN NICARAGUA THERE IS an outstanding group of mostly younger women poets. These women are currently writing the best new poetry in their country and would rank among the best new poets in Latin America. They have a good deal of contact with each other since most of them live in Managua. (Mariana Sanson lives in the provinces and Gioconda Belli lives in Costa Rica, along with Michele Najlis, another fine young Nicaraguan poet). It is important to note that the group has been encouraged by more established writers such as Luis Rocha and Pablo Antonio Cuadra. Both of these writers were on the staff of "La Prensa," the only opposition newspaper allowed by the Somoza government. A recent issue of the paper devoted several pages of its literary supplement to poems by many of the women poets.

Some of these women work at jobs ranging from secretaries to journalists. Some of the women have many family responsibilities. It seems these women have the problem of most women writers everywhere, that is finding the time to write. But in Nicaragua an additional obstacle was the potentially volatile political situation which affected almost everyone in the country. Many of these women joined the growing political protest against a strong-arm dictatorship of almost half a century. Some of these poets were exiled and some have been imprisoned for their political activities.

Their poetry varies in themes; among them social protest, concerns of women, and a search for identity. Their work is only beginning to be recognized in Latin America. Gioconda Belli won the 1978 Casa de Las Americas Poetry prize in Cuba.

Grupo nicaragüense:

Mariana Sanson

No he oído el golpe
que ha dado mi puerta
al cerrarse.
Me tendí en la cama
y dibujé palabras
que había recogido fuera.
Tomando de la mano
a cada una,
les permití salir
sin hacer ruido.

The Nicaraguan Group:

Mariana Sanson

I didn't hear the door
slam when it closed.
I lay down on the bed
and sketched words
I had gathered outside.
Taking each one by the hand
I let them leave
without making any noise.

Translated by Nora Wieser

Cuando Dios estaba
doblando el cielo
para guardarlo,
los ángeles
ayudaron de prisa.
Les estaba cansando
sostenerlo.

When God was
folding up the sky
to put it away,
the angels
hurried to help.
They were tired
of holding it up.

Translated by Nora Wieser

Grupo nicaragüense:

Lygia Guillén

UNA TRISTEZA QUE YA ME CONOCÍA

Sin compañía ya atardeciendo
frente a la jaula del oso polar
(con rocas pintadas de blanco
para simular hielo de polo norte a sur)
se vino desde la piel del animal
una tristeza que ya me conocía
con alas inseguras se posó
en el dorso de mi mano
me fué pasando su color
hasta dejarme como una roca
pintada de blanco
que quiere ser algo

The Nicaraguan Group:

Lygia Guillén

A SADNESS WHICH ALREADY KNEW ME

No one near me getting late
facing the polar bear cage
(with white rocks painted
to look like ice from the north or
south pole)
from the skin of the animal
came a sadness that already knew me
with unsure wings landing
on the back of my hand
slowly filtering me its color
until I'm left like a rock
painted white
wanting to be something

Translated by Nora Wieser

115

Grupo nicaragüense:

Vidaluz Meneses

CUANDO YO ME CASÉ

Cuando yo me casé
la Capilla era chiquita
y Monseñor recitó los salmos de rigor:

> "Que sea hacendosa como Martha
> prudente como Raquel,
> de larga vida y prolífera como Sarah."

Y heme aquí tenue sombra de Martha,
martillando la máquina de escribir en la oficina
después de los afanes del hogar,
callando la protesta fútil "silenciosa Raquel"
transcurriendo mi vida interminable como un río
para completar a Sarah.

The Nicaraguan Group:

Vidaluz Meneses

WHEN I MARRIED

When I married
it was a tiny chapel.
Monsignor recited traditional psalms:

> "May you be diligent like Martha
> prudent like Rachel
> long lifed and proliferous like Sarah."

And here you have me tenuous shadow of Martha,
hammering away at the office typewriter
after the anxieties at home,
silencing the futile protest "silent Rachel"
passing away my interminable life like a river
to make Sarah complete.

Translated by Nora Wieser

ADVERTENCIAS

No le hagas mal a nadie,
el bien, cuando esté al alcance:
la medida es el largo de tu brazo.

Porque categóricamente te comprobarán
que "el que se mete a Redentor
        crucificado termina"
y al fin y al cabo, en estos tiempos
el plato de lentejas viene bien condimentado
y al alcance de todo Contadorcillo bien pagado
de C$3.000,00 para arriba
Arriba: Gerente con Post graduado de INCAE
                        Stanford o Yale.
Experto en producir el ciento por uno
        (sin alusión bíblica por supuesto).
Y conste, con formación integral.

No descuidando la bonificación anual al empleado
porque el lomo es más explotable
sobándolo a su tiempo.
-psicología industrial -comercial aplicada-

Por eso no hay que divagar, ni teorizar
prohibido idealizar, es pasado de moda o peligroso.

Marcha a tu meta
        ser un "buen partido"
            una fiel réplica humana de eficiente IBM
un "big shot"
un envidiado miembro del "jet set"
una aristocrática minoría
un Ministro sin obligaciones.
Al final sólo te recomiendo unas potentes orejeras:
Preferible no oigas tu autocondena:
                        a lo mejor todavía te afecte.

WARNINGS

Don't do ill to anyone
good, when it's within your reach
the measure is the length of your arm.

Because categorically they'll prove to you
that "he who steps in as Saviour
ends up crucified"
and in the end, these days,
a dish of lentils comes well seasoned
and within the reach of every little
well paid bookkeeper
from C$3.000,00 on up
Up: Manager, post graduate of INCAE
                    Stanford or Yale.
Expert in producing one hundred from one
      (naturally with no biblical allusions).
And of course, an integral upbringing.

Not neglecting the annual employee's bonus
because the shoulder is the most exploitable
if it's rubbed on time.
-industrial psychology - commercially applied.

That's why there's no deviating, nor theorizing,
idealizing prohibited, out of fashion or dangerous.

March to your tune
        be a "good member"
        an exact human replica of efficient IBM
a "big shot"
an envied "jet set" member
a minority aristocrat
a cabinet minister with no obligations.
In the end I recommend only some powerful earmuffs
Preferable that you don't hear your own self condemnation:
                 it may still affect you.

                       Translated by Nora Wieser

Grupo nicaragüense:

Ana Ilce

MESA

En un rincón de la casa te han dejado. Y estás allí . . .
álbum, altar, sueño de cedros, sostenida sobre tus
cuatro pilares, viéndonos con tus ojos de profunda
madera, llegar y partir. Imperturbable permaneces
allí, dando fe aún del saludo, del consejo materno,
de aquella sopa que en nuestra infancia derramamos
y que ulceró tu piel vegetal y recién hecha. Ahora
somos menos los que llegamos a tu orilla, cada vez
alrededor de vos hay más espacio, grandes huecos
que esperan quizá para la cena final a que se siente
el padre, la madre, aquellos abuelos que un día te
trajeron a esta casa para que preservaras la costumbre,
la herencia, los recuerdos. Yo me pregunto qué árbol
generoso te dio el ser, qué oscuras manos te hirieron
de muerte para darte esta vida. Porque muy dentro de
vos corre un hilo de sangre, y quizá estás triste año-
rando tu sol, tu aire, tus pájaros. Mesa abuela,
guardiana, nodriza de la infancia, déjame llegar una vez
más hasta vos y escribir sobre tu lomo endurecido, este
recuerdo de madera.

120

The Nicaraguan Group:

Ana Ilce

TABLE

They've left you in a corner. And there you stand . . .
scrapbook, altar, an illusion of cedars on your four
pillars, watching us come and go with your profound eyes
of wood. Imperturbable you stay there, giving witness
to greetings, maternal advice, soup we spilled as children
ulcerating your newly made vegetal skin. Now there are
fewer of us who come, each time there is more space
around you, great voids which wait perhaps the last
supper and father, mother, the grandparents who one day
brought you to this house for you to preserve customs,
a heritage and memories. I ask myself which generous tree
gave you life, which dark hands dealt a mortal blow.
Because deep inside you is a thread of life blood, and
perhaps you are sadly longing for your sun, the air, your
birds. Table grandmother, guardian, infant nurse, let me
come one more time and write on your hardened back this
memory of wood.

Translated by Nora Wieser

Grupo nicaragüense:

Gioconda Belli

COTIDIANO

Toda mi casa está regada por mis poemas.
Me aparecen en la cocina, en el estudio,
en el dormitorio. Están extendidos a lo
largo de mi desorden, esparciendo su dulzura
por las horas tediosas de la barrida y de
la arreglada de los cuartos, dándome ese
mensaje de que sí hay algo vivo en mí,
de que mi vitalidad está impregnada en
esos papeles donde he dejado el recuerdo
de estos momentos intensos en que yo
dejo de ser yo y me convierto en un poema.

Gioconda Belli

THE MUNDANE

My whole house is sprinkled with my poems.

They appear before me in the kitchen, in the study,
in the bedroom. They are scattered the length
of my disorder, spreading their tenderness
along the taxing hours of vacuuming and
straightening the rooms, giving me the
message something does live in me,
that my vitality is impregnated on
those papers where I've left the memory
of intense moments when I cease
to be me and I become the poem.

Translated by Nora Wieser

Grupo nicaragüense:

Rosario Murillo

POR CULPA DEL RETRATO

Te irás quedando sola
te dejarán con la palabra en la boca
la poesía abandonada sin tinta
quedarás como eco repitiéndote
nadie querrá tu mano
ni tu parlante de truenos y gemidos
ni tu sincero caminar sin cadenas
te quedarás sin carrera
apenas sostenida apenas rama
nadie querrá escucharte
porque has pintado lo oculto
las muecas las arrugas los tintes
que no quisimos ni queremos ver
lo aborrecible tan temible nuestro.

The Nicaraguan Group:

Rosario Murillo

ON ACCOUNT OF THE PICTURE

You will begin to be alone
they will leave you with the word on your mouth
poetry abandoned with no ink
like an echo repeating yourself
no one will want your hand
nor your talk of thunder and moans
nor your honest walk without chains
you'll be left with no faces
moles eyelashes or pockets
you'll have no official duties
hardly suspended, barely a limb
no one will want to listen
because you've said too much
you've painted the secrets,
the grimaces, the wrinkles, the dyes
which we didn't want or care to see
all that we detested and is so frightfully ours.

Translated by Nora Wieser

Grupo nicaragüense:

Yolanda Blanco

LLUEVE

LLUEVE
en Teotecacinte Cusmapa
en Tepesomto Cuspire Saslaya.
Grandes charcos
cubrieron los caminos del Sinecapa
el Tule Yaoya y Mayales.

Si vas a Limay llevá capote;
y también llueve en el Macuelizo
en Ciminguasca y Alcayan.

Todo es verdecito en Tisey en Totumbla.

Garúa en Guisisil.
Truena en Yeluca y Apají.
En Nandasmo temporal seguido.

Me he mojado en todo Nicaragua
ya llueve.

126

The Nicaraguan Group:

Yolanda Blanco

ITS RAINING

IT'S RAINING
in Teotecacinte Cusmapa
in Tepesomoto Cuspire Saslaya.
Big puddles
covered the roads of Sinecapa
the Tule Yaoya and Mayales.

If you go to Limay take your raincoat
and it's also raining in the Macuelizo
in Ciminguasca and Alcayan.

Everything is nice and green in Tisey in Totumbla.

It's drizzling in Guisisil
thundering in Yeluca and Apají.
In Nandasmo continual storms.

I've been soaked in all Nicaragua
it's raining now.

Translated by Nora Wieser

127

Rosario Castellanos
México
1925–1974

ON THE 7TH OF August 1974, startling news was received in Mexico City from Tel Aviv. The Mexican ambassador to Israel, Rosario Castellanos, was electrocuted in a freak accident at her residence. The accident occurred while she was plugging in a lamp. She, herself might have incorporated her death into the plot of one of her writings. The use of the mundane to heighten the universal is a characteristic of a good deal of her later poetry and prose.

The book POESÍA NO ERES TÚ (Poetry It is not You) is her selected poetry from 1948–1971. Her poems undergo a definite evolution. In the beginning the language abounds in imagery. Elements of nature provide an abundant source. In these earlier poems we find, for example, an idyllic nature in harmony with humanity's innocent state. When the innocence disappears, the natural world becomes sterile, even hostile.

Gradually we see in her poetry a process of elimination. The language becomes more direct and simple. The most minimal daily experiences are incorporated. There is an increase in the use of irony and ironic humor. One can sense in this ironic humor an escape valve. The suffering and even despair are not diminished. They are only expressed differently.

Typical of her humor in her prose is the tongue-in-cheek approach to Jorge Luis Borges in a review of his book EL INFORME DE BRODIE. She says: "Before pronouncing the name of the Borges one has to genuflect in such a way that the extreme respect one has for his work is demonstrated. The work is so important, so perfect, and so original that only those of us who lack even the most elemental mimetic capacities abstain from imitating him. Oh, and how it hurts not to be able to do it, above all when in the United States it has been declared that the literary history of that country in the last decade is divided into two eras: before and after the translation of Borges' books."[1]

One of the themes that has been literally buried in Latin American literature is the status of women as expressed by women in protest. Castellano's poetry voices a protest about the condition of women. In poems such as "Learning about things," the message of Rosario Castellanos is quite clear.

Books of Poetry

Trayectoria del Polvo	1948
Apuntes Para una Declaración de Fe	1948
El Rescate del Mundo	1952
Poemas (1953–55)	1957
Al Pie de la Letra	1959
Lívida Luz	1960
Materia Memorable	1969
Poesía no Eres Tú	1972
En la tierra de en Medio	
Otros Poemas	
Viaje Redondo	

---

1. Rosario Castellanos, EL MAR Y SUS PESCADITOS, (México: Sep Setentas) p. 162.

129

ELEGÍA

La cordillera, el aire de la altura
que bate poderoso como el ala de un águila,
la atmósfera difícil de una estrella caída,
de una piedra celeste y enfriada.

Ésta, ésta es mi patria.

Rota, yace a mis pies la estera que tejieron
entrelazando hilos de paciencia y de magia.
O voy pisando templos destruídos
o estelas en el polvo sepultadas.

He aquí el terraplén para la danza.

¿Quién dirá los silencios de mis muertos?
¿Quién llorará la ruina de mi casa?
Entre la soledad una flauta de hueso
derramando una música triste y aguda y áspera.

No hay otra palabra.

Poesía no eres Tú

✝ ELEGY

The mountain range, a gust of heights
beating powerful as an eagle's wing,
the rigorous atmosphere of a fallen star,
a stone from the sky gone cold.

This then is my country.

The mat they braided
of patience and magic lies broken at my feet.
I tread on ruined temples
or stellae buried in dust.

Here is the ramp for the dance.

Who will tell the silences of my dead?
Who will weep over the ruins of my house?
Amidst the solitude a bone flute
spilling sad sharp music.

There are no other words.

Translated by Maureen Ahern
Poesía no eres Tú

EL OTRO

¿Por qué decir nombres de dioses, astros,
espumas de un océano invisible,
polen de los jardines más remotos?
Si nos duele la vida, si cada día llega
desgarrando la entraña, si cada noche cae
convulsa, asesinada.
Si nos duele el dolor en alguien, en un hombre
al que no conocemos, pero está
presente a todas horas y es la víctima
y el enemigo y el amor y todo
lo que nos falta para ser enteros.
Nunca digas que es tuya la tiniebla,
no te bebas de un sorbo la alegría.
Mira a tu alrededor: hay otro, siempre hay otro.
Lo que él respira es lo que a ti te asfixia,
lo que come es tu hambre.
Muere con la mitad más pura de tu muerte.

Poesía no eres Tú

SOMEONE ELSE

Why utter the names of gods or stars
sea-foam of an invisible sea,
or pollen of distant gardens
if it hurts to be alive,
if each day dawns gnawing at the gut,
if each night falls, convulsed, murdered
if we hurt from the pain,
in someone we don't know,
who is always here and is the victim,
the enemy and love and everything
we need to be whole.
Never say darkness is your own,
don't drink down joy in one gulp.
Look around you: There's someone else, there's always
   someone else
Who breathes what stifles you,
who eats your hunger.
Who dies with the purest half of your death.

Translated by Maureen Ahern
Poesía no eres Tú

AMANECER

¿Qué se hace a la hora de morir? ¿Se vuelve
la cara a la pared?
¿Se agarra por los hombros al que está cerca y oye?
¿Se echa uno a correr, como el que tiene
las ropas incendiadas, para alcanzar el fin?

¿Cuál es el rito de esta ceremonia?
¿Quién vela la agonía? ¿Quién estira la sábana?
¿Quién aparta el espejo sin empañar?

Porque a esta hora ya no hay madre y deudos.

Ya no hay sollozo. Nada, más que un silencio atroz.

Todos son una faz atenta, incrédula
de hombre de la otra orilla.

Porque lo que sucede no es verdad.

Poesía no eres tú

DAWN

What do you do at the moment of dying? Do you
turn your face to the wall?
Do you grab the nearest person by the shoulders?
Do you start running to reach the end
like someone with their clothes on fire?
What are the rites for this ceremony?
What keeps the deathwatch? Who pulls up the sheet?
Who sets down the unclouded mirror?
Because at this moment there is no mother, no relatives,
no sobbing. Nothing. Only an atrocious silence.
They all comprise the eager incredulous face
of the man on the other shore.
Because what is happening is not true.

Translated by Maureen Ahern
Poesía no eres Tú

AJEDREZ

Porque éramos amigos y, a ratos, nos amábamos;
quizá para añadir otro interés
a los muchos que ya nos obligaban
decidimos jugar juegos de inteligencia.

Pusimos un tablero enfrente de nosotros:
equitativo en piezas, en valores,
en posibilidad de movimientos.
Aprendimos las reglas, les juramos respeto
y empezó la partida.

Hénos aquí, hace un siglo, sentados, meditando
encarnizadamente
cómo dar el zarpazo último que aniquile
de modo inapelable y, para siempre, al otro.

Poesía no eres Tú

136

CHESS

Because we were friends and sometime lovers;
perhaps to add one more interest
to the many we already held
we chose to play games of the mind.

We set up a board opposite each other
equally divided in pieces, in values
and possible movements.
We learned the rules, we swore to honor them
and the match began.

And here we are, sitting for centuries, meditating
ferociously
how to deal the one last blow
that will totally annihilate
the other, once and forever.

Translated by Maureen Ahern
Poesía no eres Tú

SE HABLA DE GABRIEL

Como todos los huéspedes mi hijo me estorbaba
ocupando un lugar que era mi lugar,
existiendo a deshora,
haciéndome partir en dos cada bocado.

Fea, enferma, aburrida
lo sentía crecer a mis expensas,
robarle su color a mi sangre, añadir
un peso y un volumen clandestinos
a mi modo de estar sobre la tierra.

Su cuerpo me pidió nacer, cederle el paso;
darle un sitio en el mundo,
la provisión de tiempo necesaria a su historia.

Consentí. Y por la herida en que partió, por esa
hemorragia de su desprendimiento
se fue también lo último que tuve
de soledad, de yo mirando tras de un vidrio.

Quedé abierta, ofrecida
a las visitaciones, al viento, a la presencia.

Poesía no eres Tú

138

SPEAKING OF GABRIEL

Like all guests my son disturbed me
occupying a place that was mine,
existing inopportunely
making me split each mouthful in two.

Ugly, sick, bored
I felt him grow at my expense,
rob my blood of its color and
secretly add a weight and a volume
to my way of being upon this earth.

His body begged me to make way for him
to give him a place in the world
to provide the necessary time for his history.

I consented. When he departed through that wound,
through that loosening hemorrhage
the last of my loneliness, of looking out behind a glass
flowed out.

I became open, to visitations,
to the wind,
to presence.

Translated by Maureen Ahern
Poesía no eres Tú

MEDITACIÓN EN EL UMBRAL

No, no es la solución
tirarse bajo un tren como la Ana de Tolstoy
ni apurar el arsénico de Madame Bovary
ni aguardar en los páramos de Avila la visita
del ángel con venablo
antes de liarse el manto a la cabeza
y comenzar a actuar.

Ni concluir las leyes geométricas, contando
las vigas de la celda de castigo
como lo hizo Sor Juana. No es la solución
escribir, mientras llegan las visitas,
en la sala de estar de la familia Austen
ni encerrarse en el ático
de alguna residencia de la Nueva Inglaterra
y soñar, con la Biblia de los Dickinson,
debajo de una almohada de soltera.

Debe haber otro modo que no se llame Safo
ni Messalina ni María Egipcíaca
ni Magdalena ni Clemencia Isaura.

Otro modo de ser humano y libre.

Otro modo de ser.

Poesía no eres Tú

MEDITATION ON THE BRINK

No, it's not a solution
to throw oneself under a train like Tolstoy's Anna
or gulp down Madame Bovary's arsenic
or await on the barren heights of Avila the visit
of the angel with the fiery dart
before binding the cloak back over one's head
and starting to act.

Nor to deduce laws of geometry counting
the beams of one's solitary confinement cell
like Sor Juana did. It's not a solution
to write, while the company arrives,
in the Austen family living room
or to shut oneself up in the attic
of some New England house
and dream, with the Dickinson's family Bible
under a spinster pillow.

There must be another way that's not named Sappho
or Messalina or Mary of Egypt
or Magdalene or Clemencia Isaura.[1]

Another way to be human and free.

Another way to be.

Translated by Maureen Ahern
Poesía no eres Tú

---

1. Clemence Isaure, a 15th century French woman whose name was symbolic
in poetry celebrating the Virgin.

LECCIONES DE COSAS

Me enseñaron las cosas equivocadamente
los que enseñan las cosas:
los padres, el maestro, el sacerdote
pues me dijeron: tienes que ser buena.

Basta ser bueno. Al bueno se le da
un dulce, una medalla, todo el amor, el cielo.

Y ser bueno es muy fácil. Basta abatir los párpados
para no ver y no juzgar lo que hacen
los otros, porque no es de tu incumbencia.

Basta no abrir los labios para no protestar
cuando alguno te empuje porque, o no quiso herirte
o no pudo evitarlo
o Dios está probando el temple de tu alma.

De cualquier modo, pues, cuando te ocurra el mal
hay que aceptarlo, agradecerlo incluso
pero no devolverlo. Y no preguntes
por qué. Porque los buenos
no son inquisitivos.

Y dar. Si tienes una capa córtala
en dos y entrega la mitad al otro
-aunque el otro no sea más que un coleccionista
de mitades de capa. Eso es asunto suyo
y tu mano derecha debe ignorar . . . etcétera.

Y recibir con ambas mejillas, eso sí.

No siempre serán golpes.

A veces será el ramo de flores que suscita
fiebre de heno. A veces el marisco
que te produce alergia.

LEARNING ABOUT THINGS

They taught me things all wrong,
the ones who teach things:
my parents, the teacher, the priest.
You have to be good they told me.

It's enough to be good. Because the good person
gets a piece of candy, a medal, all the love, and heaven, too.

And it's very easy to be good. All you have to do is lower
your eyelids
in order not to see or judge what others do
because it does not pertain to you.

You just don't have to open your mouth not to protest
when someone shoves you because they didn't
mean to hurt you or
they couldn't help it or
because God is testing the mettle of your soul

But anyhow when something bad does happen to you
you just accept it, even be grateful for it
but not return it. And don't ask why.
Because good people
are not curious.

And you have to give. If you own a cape, cut it in two
and give one half to someone else
—even though that someone else may very well be
a collector of other halves of capes.
That's his business and your right hand must ignore
what your left hand . . . . etc. etc.

And you must turn both cheeks. Ah, Yes,

They won't always be blows.

It may be a bouquet of flowers that gives you
hay fever. Or the seafood that gives
you an allergy.

A veces el elogio
que, si no es falso, humilla de raíz
y que si es falso, ofende. Tú perdona
que es lo que hacen los buenos.

Obedecía. Se sabe: la obediencia
es la virtud mayor.

Y pasaron los años
y yo era la piedra de tropiezo contra
la que chocaba el distraído o,
si mejor emplazada, punching bag
en el que ejercitaban su destreza los fuertes.

A veces me ponía a hacer "viva la flor"
con mis cartas del naipe y llovía la gracia
indiferentemente sobre mis amigos
y los que eran amigos de mis amigos, es
decir, mis enemigos.

Y me senté a esperar la medalla o el dulce
y la sonrisa, el premio, por fin, en este mundo.

Y sólo vi desprecio por mi debilidad,
odio por haber sido el instrumento,
de la maldad ajena.

¿Con qué derecho yo quería santificarme
utilizando vicios o carencias
de los demás? ¿Por qué yo me elegí
como única elegida
y era en el mecanismo como el grano de arena
que paraliza toda función? Y, paralíticos,
los activos pensaban. Y yo era la causa
eficiente de aquellos pensamientos
y no había para mí sino condenación.

sometimes praise
which if not false, cuts to the quick
and if it is false, offends. Forgive
because that is what good people do.

So I obeyed. For it is known that
obedience is the greatest virtue.

So the years went by
and I was that stumbling block
the absent-minded tripped over or better yet,
a punching bag
the strong tried out their skill on.

Sometimes at cards I would deal a royal flush
but this cleverness rained indifferently
upon my friends
and my friends' friends,
I mean my enemies.

So then I sat down to wait for the medal
the piece of candy and the smile, in short
the prize in this world.

But all I saw was scorn for my own weakness.
Hate for having been the tool
of others' malice.

Since when did I have the right to want to canonize
myself using others' vices or defects?
Why was I electing myself
the only chosen one?
Why was I that grain of sand in the works
that paralyzes every function?
Paralyzed, the doers were thinking.

And I was the efficient cause of their thoughts.
So for me there was only contempt.

Hasta que comprendí. Y me hice un tornillo
bien aceitado con el cual la máquina
trabaja ya satisfactoriamente.

Un tornillo. No tengo
ningún nombre específico ni ningún atributo
según el cual poder calificarme
como mejor o peor o más o menos útil
que los otros tornillos.

Si tuviera que hacer mi apología
ante alguien (que no hay nadie, nunca hubo
ningún testigo de lo que acontece)
diría que estuve en mi lugar y que
giré en la dirección correcta y a la velocidad
requerida y con la frecuencia necesaria.

Y que no procuré ni que me reemplazaran
antes de tiempo, ni me permitieran
seguir cuando había sido declarada inservible.

Y, antes de terminar, quiero que quede
bien claro que no hice nada de lo que hice
por humildad. ¿Acaso los tornillos
son humildes? ¡Ridículo! Y que, menos aún,
mi conducta se entiende merced a la esperanza.

No, ya hace mucho tiempo que el cielo es un factor
que no entra en mis cálculos.

Conformidad, tal vez. Lo que de ningún modo
en un tornillo, como yo, es un mérito
sino, a lo sumo, es una condición.

Poesía no eres Tú

146

Until I finally understood. So I made myself
into a well-oiled cog with which the machine
now turns perfectly.

A cog. I don't have
any specific name or any attribute
according to which I can classify myself
as any better or any worse or even more or less useful
than any of the other cogs.

If I should have to come up with a justification
for someone (and there isn't anyone — there never was any
witness for what happens)
I would say that I was in my place
that I spun in the right direction at
the required speed and the required frequency.

That I never tried to get them to replace me
ahead of time nor to allow me to continue once
I had been declared useless.

Before I finish I want to make it perfectly clear
that I did none of these things
out of humility. Since when are cogs humble?

Ridiculous! And that certainly
my behavior cannot be attributed to hope.

No, for a long time now heaven is a factor
that doesn't figure in my calculations.

Conformity? Perhaps. Which in a cog, like me
is not in any way a merit,
but rather, at best, a condition.

Translated by Maureen Ahern
Poesía no eres Tú

Eunice Odio

Costa Rica
1922–1974

EUNICE ODIO WAS ARRANGING an edition of her collected poetry when she died in 1974. The book was completed by her friends. It is published by the Editorial Universitaria Centroamericana in San Jose, Costa Rica, and entitled *TERRITORIO DEL ALBA* (Dawn's Territory). The book contains poems spanning the years 1946–972. Some of this poetry was published in separate volumes which today would not all be readily accessible to anyone but the diligent researcher. Yet a great deal of work needs to be done. Her voice is, indeed, one of the most original in contemporary Latin American poetry.

She seems to wave a magic wand over reality and create new worlds closely aligned with nature in a delicate, often diminutive unfolding of dramas. As readers we can follow her to these hitherto unexplored regions through language and feeling. She helps us by heightening our sensitivity and unbridling our imagination. Even then, some of her imagery is extremely hermetic but it intrigues and captivates.

In *TERRITORIO DEL ALBA* one finds an incongruity between her poetry and the description of her person which at the end of the book takes the form of commentaries by people (all men) who knew her. She was an extraordinary beauty. There seems evidence of a tendency toward self-destruction. Extremely outspoken, she renounced very early any affiliation with her native country because she could not tolerate the provincialism and intrigues of the literary circles in Costa Rica. She lived in Nicaragua, Guatemala, El Salvador, Cuba, the U.S. and finally Mexico.

148

It was in Mexico City that she was found in her apartment on May 22, 1974. Reputedly, she had died eight days earlier in circumstances that are still unclear. The solitude of such a death is ironical in a society that prides itself on friendships and interpersonal relationships. Yet no bitterness, rancor or profound disillusionment is evident in *TERRITORIO DEL ALBA*. On the contrary, a great many of the poems are dedicated to or about friends. They reveal the tenderness and love of a very sensitive woman. An example is a prose poem "A letter to Carlos Pellicer."[1] She gives him, among other wonders, a "tablespoon of swallows from Chichen-Itza," . . . "a glass full of butterflies that never sleep" . . . "a woman found in the fire whom no one could understand." She ends the poem by saying, "P.S. I had forgotten to give you all the horizon and its consequences." For the attentive reader of Eunice Odio's poetry, one horizon is an understatement. She has left us much more.

Books of Poetry

Territorio del Alba	1946–1954
Los Elementos Terrestres	1948
Tránsito de Fuego	1957
Pasto de Sueños	1953–1971
Últimos Poemas	1967-1972
Territorio Del Alba	1974

---

1. Carlos Pellicer is a contemporary Mexican poet. This poem is found on pages 200-201 of *TERRITORIO DEL ALBA*.

3

Escucha ese silencio,

Es un silencio anclado,

es un sesgo de rosa,
es un pliegue dormido de los ańgeles.

Escucha ese silencio
que se pega a tu carne,

Es un pasar de humo a tu costado.

Madre soledad se vence del lado de los bosques,
de los sueños con Sol
de los estados de las flores.

Territorio del Alba

Listen to that silence,

It's an anchored silence,

it's the serenity of a rose
it's a sleeping fold of angels.

Listen to that silence
sticking to your flesh,

It's smoke passing by your side.

Mother solitude leans toward the forests,
toward dreams with the Sun,
toward the seasons of flowers.

> Translated by Priscilla Joslin
> *Territorio del Alba*

RETRATOS DEL CORAZÓN

A Olga Kochen

Antes de enamorarne de mujer alguna,
jugué mi corazón al azar y me lo ganó
la violencia.

Jose Eustacio Rivera

I.

Sabiéndolo cautivo del azar
abandoné mi corazón al viento
y éste lo dio a la tempestad.

Pero volvió . . . sabía que volvería.

Yo presiento que un día volvió del fuego,
a ser fuego del cielo ensimismado.

Se incorporó a mi carne,
ya desatado fruto del relámpago.

II.

Sale al rostro fugaz sin compañía.
Nadie lo ve llegar,

al polvo dar aliento,
pasto al sueño,

ser dominio del día y movimiento.

III.

Ser lo que sube a espaldas de la aurora,
ser la actitud del huerto
y no la mano ardiente que lo toca.

IV.

No habita la mañana,
no marcha al son del cielo,
a la cabeza va del claro día.

PORTRAITS OF THE HEART

To Olga Kochen

Before falling in love with any woman,
I gambled my heart and lost to violence.

José Eustacio Rivera

I.

Knowing it was a prisoner of chance
I abandoned my heart to the wind
which gave it to the storm.

But it returned . . . I knew it would.

I sense that one day it returned from the fire,
to become the flame of an introverted sky.

It joined with my flesh,
already an unleashed fruit of lightning.

II.

It appears on the fleeting face unaccompanied.
No one sees it arrive,

give spirit to dust,
nourishment to dream

become day and movement's dominion

III.

Become that which arises behind dawn,
mood of a garden
and not the burning hand which touches it.

IV.

It doesn't live in mornings,
or march to sky sounds,
it's the lead on a clear day.

153

De su presencia quedan,
en el campo,
rastros como banderas.

Compañero del alba
no dentro de ella va,

en el gran río terrestre de todo lo perdido,

con ella va, en su ruido,
hacia la ausencia.

V.
Presencia fue del alma,
perpetua faz, "incombustible llama,"
fuego es y al fuego será tornada.

VI.
Lo interrumpe una lágrima
y del cielo no queda ni una lámpara.
-Cielo vertido en otra edad del alma-.
No hay nadie en mi criatura,
nadie me habla en secreto . . .

Sólo un testigo matinal
de lo que fue vertido en el silencio.

VII.
Me espío.
¿A dónde va mi corazón?

Cae de Dios con un relámpago.

VIII.
Angel interno . . .
Detrás de Dios se oculta.

Lo anda buscando el sueño.

Traces of its presence remain
like flags
along the countryside.

Daybreak's companion,
it doesn't travel within it

on the great earth river of all that is lost,

moving with it, within its sounds
toward absence.

V.
It was the presence of the soul,
a perpetual face, "fireproof flame,"
it is fire and shall return to fire.

VI.
A tear interrupts
and no lamp is left in the sky.

-A sky formed in another time of the soul-

There is no one in me,
no one speaks to me in secrecy . . .

Only one witness from the morning —
that which was poured into silence.

VII.
I spy on myself.
Where is my heart going?

Falling from God on a lightning bolt.

VIII.
Internal angel . . .
Hiding behind God.

A dream is searching for it.

IX.
Afirma.
¿Qué afirmación lo hace girar,
ser el lenguaje

de una historia secreta?

La afirmación del aire.

Pasto de Sueños

IX.
Affirming.

What affirmation makes it turn,
become the language

of a secret history?

An affirmation of the air.

Translated by Priscilla Joslin
Pasto de Sueños

Amanda Berenguer
Uruguay

AMANDA BERENGUER LIVES IN Montevideo. With her husband, José Pedro Díaz, an outstanding literary critic and novelist, Amanda shares a love for literature, for the power of language, for the potential in human expression. They are both dedicated to their writing and they are respectful and proud of the other's accomplishments. They have shared with each other many years of development in their work. At one time they had a small printing press, "La Galatea," which turned out exquisite editions of poetry in limited numbers, all carefully executed with the dedication that is characteristic of both writers. Their house has always been a gathering place for writers that are friends of long standing. They have met with friends over the years in the best tradition of the Spanish literary "tertulia" or gathering, serving one another both as critics and as stimulants for new ideas.

Amanda Berenguer's tremendously inquisitive mind is evidenced in the evolution of her poetry. In her early poetry there is, for example, the traditional elegy or ballad form. Beginning with her book QUEHACERES E INVENCIONES 1963 (Duties and Inventions) the images become more abstract; illogical enumeration is frequently utilized to denote underlying themes of death, the absurdity of existence or the search for people's place in the order of things. Her curiosity has motivated a continual exploration of new possibilities for expression. She made a record in 1973 called DICCIONES (Dictions) which she herself describes as "recreating the poem with the voice . . . I thought: is there another way to know poetry? The poem was already written and I threw myself on it to say it, distort it, shout it, I don't know, to invent it anew . . . If I wanted to do it again it would be different. No version is equal to another." The experience of the record she says "creates (the poem) anew, gives it another space and time coincidental with the real time and space . . . I have always been inordinately concerned with the forms of communication. I've always moved in the realm of poetry and until now I have used the printed book to reach out."[1]

In her latest book COMPOSICIÓN DE LUGAR 1976 (Composition of Place)[2] the central theme is the sunset on nineteen different dates in time. Each poem has three versions: the first is in traditional free verse. The second version has key words or derivatives of key words from the first version arranged in patterns or formulas. The third and last version is a visual arrangement which interweaves key letters or words in varying sizes and densities. This version is not translatable since the letters of the words are vital to the pattern formation. In the "Posición" (Position), a kind of prologue, she refers to the third version of the poems as parallel in their flowing or fleeting aspect, to the setting of the sun or even to our own position of flux in the universe. "The plasticity of the words in this graphic arrangement," she says, "makes the space they occupy on the page a veritable Moebius strip,[3] a dynamic and quiet source that consumes and creates itself at the same time." She ends by saying: "The word is thus a paradoxical mobile suspended in the air, which goes from the song to the shout of the page."

Books of Poetry

Elegía por la Muerte de Paul Valéry	1945
El Río	1952
La Invitación	1957
Contracanto	1961
Quehaceres e Invenciones	1963
Declaración Conjunta	1964
Materia Prima	1966
Dicciones (Record)	1973
Composición de Lugar	1976
Poesía (1949–1979)	1979

---

1. The Spanish also means to take stock of, as in a place or a situation.
2. Interview by Jorge Ruffinelli in *Marcha*, June 30, 1973.
3. Geometry. A strip of paper or other material which is given a half twist and then joined at the ends, thus having only one side.

COMUNICACIONES

Urge el pensamiento conectando
¿errata? ¿paréntesis? ¿qué signo?
¿escuchan?
(La claridad del lenguaje
tiene apenas
la intensidad ambigua del poniente)
Estamos aquí, lanzados a la noche
terrestre, apretujados,
aquí, en la noche terrestre, aquí,
en la noche terrestre.
De nuevo el hilo,
el cable roto, el deslumbrante
cortocircuito.
¿No oyen? ¿No se oye?
Palabras mías, insensatas,
hechas de furor y de locura,
cuantiosa tesitura negra
a borbotones desbordándose
hacia dentro, hacia
el fondo
interpolado de rígidas luciérnagas.

Tiembla y destella, hace señales,
todas son huellas de la eternidad,
enumeradas y prolijas,
cuernos de caza, al mundo,
aullidos de perros, está el desierto,
toques de peligro, inútilmente,
pasos cambiados, ¿dónde?,
campanas para niebla, una piel fosforescente,
pedidos de auxilio, y envenenada,
sirenas de patrulleros, llamando,

COMMUNICATIONS

The thought urges connecting
does one feel? someone between the lines?
erratum? parenthesis? what sign?
are they listening?
(the clarity of the language
has barely
the ambiguous intensity of dusk)
We are here, thrown to the earthly night,
squeezed
here, in the earthly night, here
in the earthly night.
Once again the thread,
the broken cable, the dazzling
shortcircuit.
Don't they hear? Can't it be heard?
My words, senseless,
made of furor and madness,
copious black
bubbling ever inwardly
towards
the bottom
mixing with rigid fireflies.

Trembling, exploding, making signs,
traces of eternity,
enumerated and prolix,
horns of the hunt, to the world,
howling dogs, the desert,
sounds of danger, uselessly
changed steps, where?
fog horns, a phosphorescent skin,
pleas for help, and poisoned.
police sirens, calling

gritos de alarma, solo, solo, solo,
bocinas de ambulancias, se hace tarde,
quiero saber si se hace tarde.

Un código de emergencia,
un vaso de agua, un hueso
para la inteligencia,
un alfabeto de clave radioactiva,
o telepática, o nuclear,
o una sustancia de amor
para esta extrema ubicación,
25 de abril de 1963, otoño,
en mi casa, hemisferio austral,
aparentemente a la deriva.

Quehaceres e Invenciones

162

a armed screams, alone, alone, alone,
ambulance sirens, it's getting late,
I want to know if it's getting late.

An emergency code,
a glass of water, a bone
for intelligence,
an alphabet of radioactive clues,
or telepathic or nuclear,
or a substance of love
for this extreme location,
25 of April 1963, autumn,
at my house, southern hemisphere,
apparently adrift.

Translated by Priscilla Joslin
Quehaceres e Invenciones

TAREA DOMÉSTICA

Sacudo las telarañas del cielo
desmantelado
con el mismo utensilio
de todos los días,
sacudo el polvo obsecuente
de los objetos regulares, sacudo
el polvo, sacudo el polvo
de astros, cósmico abatimiento
de siempre, siempremuerta caricia
cubriendo el mobiliario terrestre,
sacudo puertas y ventanas, limpio
sus vidrios para ver más claro,
barro el piso tapado de deshechos,
de hojas arrugadas, de ceniza,
de migas, de pisadas,
de huesos relucientes,
barro la tierra, más abajo, la tierra,
y voy haciendo un pozo
a la medida de las circunstancias.

Quehaceres e Invenciones

HOUSEWORK

I brush the spider webs from the dismantled sky
with the same everyday utensil,
I brush the obedient dust
off the regular objects, I brush
the dust, I brush the astral
dust, the usual cosmic depression
everdead caress
covering the earth's furniture.
I dust doors and windows, clean their
panes to see more clearly,
I sweep the littered floor,
crumpled leaves, ashes,
crumbs, footprints,
gleaming bones,
I sweep the earth, farther and farther down
and I'm slowly making a pit
to fit the circumstances.

Translated by Priscilla Joslin
Quehaceres e Invenciones

TABLA DEL DOS

Tengo dos veces veinte de juventud
aprendí la tabla de multiplicar por dos
de vida memorizo asimilo cada sustancia
crezco sobremanera me reproduzco
por partenogénesis por división espontánea
por alegre decisión a todo color
y en rápidas tomas de poder
tengo dos veces la que era
dos veces el mar revuelto el bosque
de aparecidos el campo surcado
la calle con barricadas
la casa hirviendo a fuego vivo dos veces
cuatro palabras básicas ocho palomas
mensajeras dieciséis salvoconductos
trienta y dos teléfonos sesenta y cuatro
portavoces multiplicando hechos concretos
bien alimentados sueños dados de alta
amor cosificado
tengo el cociente aprendiz de brujo
innumerable
llega a su límite la membrana exterior
la piel del continente se abre comienza
el mundo dos de aduana franca.

Materia Prima

THE TWO TIMES TABLE

I'm two times twenty
I learned to multiply by two
I memorize assimilate each life substance
I grow inordinately, I reproduce myself
by parthenogenesis, by spontaneous division
by lively decision in all colors
and with quick seizures of power
I have two times what I was
two times an unruly sea a forest
with phantoms furrowed land
barricaded street
two times the house boiling on high flame
four basic words eight messenger pigeons
sixteen safe conduct passes
thirty two telephones sixty four
megaphones multiplying concrete facts
well nourished dreams pronounced cured
love thingualized
I have the sorcerer's apprentice quotient
numberless
the exterior membrane reaches its limits
the hide of the continent opens up begins
the world by two duty-free borders.

Translated by Nora Wieser
Materia Prima

INVENTARIO SOLEMNE

A María Inés Silva Vila
y Carlos Maggi

Incluso el galápago fuera de hora,
y el pez de plata antigua,
y la corona seca, las pulseras,
y el anillo con incrustaciones
del reino vegetal.
También una caja de madera
con la araña, la escolopendra
y el escorpión
acomodados para regalo.
En una jaula los pájaros
revoloteando hacia los cuatro puntos
privativos del cielo casa escaparate,
mientras caen las plumas lentamente
a igual velocidad
y se depositan sobre las hojas del patio
de una estación vacía, comprendida.
Además una cueva, o nacimiento,
y sus bisontes cuaternarios
en una tácita cacería urbana.
Añadiendo las boas blancas o negras
de avestruz o marabú, contorsionadas
sobre un charco de naftalina.
Item, un cuero de gato montés
copulando con una garza rosada
apretados entre los sombreros
y las aves del paraíso.
Item, recuerdos.
Item, objetos chicos, lisos y pastosos,

SOLEMN INVENTORY*

To María Inés Silva Vila
and Carlos Maggi

Including the Galapago turtle out of time
and the fish of ancient silver
and the dried crown, the bracelets
and the ring with incrustations
from the vegetal kingdom.
Also a wooden box
with the spider, the centipide
and the scorpion
prepared as a gift.
In a cage the birds
fluttering toward the four private
points of the sky-house-show-window
while their feathers fall slowly
all at the same rate
landing on the patio leaves
of an empty comprehensive season.
In addition, a cave, or nativity
and its quaternary bison
in a tacit urban hunt.
Also the white or black ostrich or
marabou boas twisted on a
puddle of naphthalene.
Item, the hide of a mountain lion
copulating with a pink heron
squeezed between the hats
and the birds of paradise.
Item, memories.
Item, small objects smooth and doughy,

*A note from the author explains that solemn inventory is the term a notary
uses for a dead person's belongings.

169

amasados con menstruación y agua de rosas.
Item, materiales inservibles.
Item, carne y huesos.
Item, cosas para después y nunca.
Item más, el libro de actas, puntual, al día.

Materia Prima

kneaded with menstruation and rose water.
Item, useless materials.
Item, flesh and bones.
Item, things for afterwards and never,
More item, the minutes book, punctual, up to date.

Translated by Nora Wieser
Materia Prima

PONIENTE SOBRE EL MAR DEL
SÁBADO 4 DE MARZO DE 1972

(primera versión)

El incendio se propaga
frío resplandeciente con la calma
de un estado de conciencia
detrás del mar intacto
pardo animal escamoso
todo de acero grabado
frontera última del día de hoy
desaparecieron los fuegos iniciales
los focos los destellos
el cielo que gritaba
consignas visionarias
deslumbra una idea fija total
desnuda incombustible
clavando el resplandor exacto
en el linde donde comienza
lo que ignoramos.

Composición de Lugar

THE SUNSET ON THE SEA
SATURDAY THE 4TH OF MARCH, 1972

(first version)

The fire advances
cold, resplendent with the calm
of a conscience state
behind the sea intact
gray, scaly animal
all etched in steel
last frontier of today's day
initial flames have disappeared
focuses light rays
a sky that shouted
visionary watchwords
dazzles a total fixed idea
naked incombustible
nailing the exact splendor
in the border where
everything we ignore begins.

Translated by Nora Wieser
Composición de Lugar

EL INCENDIO SE PROPAGA *(segunda versión)*	THE FIRE ADVANCES *(second version)*
I burn	ardo
arch	arco
zero	cero
frontier	frontera
route last	ruta última
border	linde
begin	comienza
wreaths	ramos
wreaths	ramos
wreaths	ramos
Composición de Lugar	Translated by Nora Wieser and the author *Composición de Lugar*

174

MAR PARDO ANIMAL ESCAMOSO ACERO GRABADO FRONTERA ÚLTIMA LINDE DONDE COMIENZA LO QUE IGNORAMOS

(tercera versión)   *(third version)*

Blanca Varela
Perú

BLANCA VARELA IS A NATIVE of Lima, and has lived in Paris and New York. She was in contact with Parisian existentialists and with New York's kaleidoscopic fast pace. These two experiences melded with others and with her own innate way of being result in a forceful poetry about existence. Humankind in her view are abandoned beings. They are left with their own inadequacies floundering in a sometimes, tedious, often painful existence. At times her poetry is tinged with irony, sometimes humorous, often irreverent.

She is very modest about her work; it is one among many concerns in her life. She refuses to publish any of her poems until she feels the language has achieved all its potential with the message. She writes about creating poetry:

> a poem
> like a great battle
> thrusts me on this sand
> no other enemy than myself

myself
and this immense,
immense air of words

We see here the poet as a potential obstacle to the poem; perhaps in the
sense of being bound by norm and tradition. It is evident in her poetry
that she seeks to free language from conventional associations, in the
manner of surrealism. Her images are often irrational yet piercing in their
sadness or violence. The enumeration in her poetry draws its force from its
sense of chaos. Time and history in many of her poems have a mythical
quality. These elements and others merit further study by literary critics,
since it is difficult to deny the power of her language.

Books of Poetry

Ese Puerto Existe	1959
Luz de Día	1963
Valses y Otras Falsas Confesiones	1972

MADONNA

La que había visto todo se volvió de perfil, orgullosa y fortalecida. Sobre el lecho se incorporó la madre y ofreció el hijo, envuelto como una crisálida, a los postreros rayos del sol.

Al mismo tiempo el ama acercaba el seno henchido y moreno al labio virgen del recién llegado, pero él dormía, indiferente al calor del sol y al misterio del primer beso.

Un crítico severo hubiera reclamado un fulgor de sangre en el entarimado de porcelana, y que el triángulo de cielo de la ventana hubiera sido más azul, más cielo.

Y además, aquel niño ya crecido, al centro de todo, oraba de una manera extraña, uniendo las plantas de los pies como un simio.

La arquitectura era limpia pero banal, con algo de templo y de mercado. Escaleras inútiles, ventanas que aspiraban la oscuridad a borbotones, arcos bajos como tumbas, escaños desocupados y cortinajes anudados con ira.

Y luego, cruzando el tiempo, el cortejo de mujeres con sus dones y secretos a cuestas. Estaban todas. La que lucía el vientre como una hogaza dura y rubia bajo la gasa mortecina. La madre de aquel párvulo que se protegía del milagro a la sombra de la cadera familiar y opulenta. La dueña de la trenza todavía infantil y del seno obviamente maduro. Y entre ellas, apartada, la célibe: sabia como una abuela, poderosa de brazos y ensimismada frente a la ventana.

De espaldas a la escena la más grave, la más dulce de todas. Con el niño extraño y crecido entre los brazos parecía saberlo todo. Amor en sus ojos extraviados, ceguera y luz en el rostro del infante rollizo.

Al fondo, huyendo del lugar, un anciano trepaba penosamente las escaleras. En lo alto lo esperaba una dama, noble de porte y vestido, que lo ayudaba gentilmente a trasponer el umbral que le correspondía.

Luz de Día

MADONNA

The one who'd seen it all turned her face away. She was
proud, made prouder. The mother sitting up in bed, holding
her baby like a cocoon to the sun's last rays.

Just then the nurse brought a dark, swollen breast to the
infant's lips. But he was asleep caring nothing for the sun,
the mystery of a first kiss.

A demanding person might complain about a fleshy tone
in the tile floor, the window's triangle of sky should be more
blue, more like the sky.

And not just that — the child, center of attention, crying
so strangely, the soles of his feet together like a monkey!

The architecture clean, but nothing new — part temple,
part market. Stairs that lead nowhere, windows drowning,
breathing in darkness, tomblike arches, empty benches, curtains
knotted in anger.

And then, cutting across time, the procession of women
with the virtues and secrets of their shoulders. They're all
there. The one whose belly shone like a loaf of hard, white
bread beneath her shroud. The mother with a child behind
her full, comforting hip, protecting himself from the miracle.
The married woman with the childish braid and the conspicuosly
mature breasts. And among them, but standing apart, the virgin:
wise as a grandmother, with powerful arms, at the window lost
in thought.

Her back to the scene, the gravest, the sweetest of all.
The strange child in her arms, she seems to know everything.
Love in her rolling eyes, blindness and light in the boy's
plump face.

And in the background, fleeing, an old man climbs pain-
fully up the stairs. At the top stands a woman, beautifully
dressed, ready to help him gently through the right door.

Translated by Marti Moody
Luz de Día

Tal vez en primavera
Deja que pase esta sucia estación de hollín y
    lágrimas hipócritas.
Hazte fuerte. Guarda miga sobre miga. Haz
    una fortaleza
de toda la corrupción y el dolor.
Llegado el tiempo tendrás alas y un rabo
    fuerte de toro
o de elefante para liquidar todas las dudas
    todas las
moscas, todas las desgracias.

Baja del árbol.
Mírate en el agua. Aprende a odiarte como a
    tí mismo.
Eres tú. Rudo, pelado, primero en cuatro patas,
    luego
en dos, después en ninguna.
Arrástrate hasta el muro, escucha la música
    entre las
piedrecitas. Llámalas siglos, huesos, cebollas.
Da lo mismo. Las palabras, los nombres, no tienen importancia.
Escucha la música. Sólo la música.

Valses y Otras Falsas Confesiones

Perhaps in the spring
Let this season of soot and hypocrite tears pass.
Make yourself strong. Save crumb upon crumb. Build
     a fortress.
of all the corruption and pain.
When the time comes you'll have wings and the
     strong tail of a bull
or of an elephant to dissolve all the doubts
     all the
flies, all the adversities.

Come down from the tree.
Look at yourself in the water. Learn to hate yourself
     as yourself.
It is you. Crude, hairy, first on four legs,
     afterwards
on two, then on none.
Drag yourself to the wall, listen to the music
     among the
small stones. Call them centuries, bones, onions.
It's all the same. The words, the names don't
matter. Listen to the music. Only
the music.

Translated by Nora Wieser
Valses y Otras Falsas Confesiones

VALS DEL ÁNGELUS I

Ve lo que has hecho de mí, la santa más pobre del museo, la de la última sala, junto a las letrinas, la de la herida negra como un ojo bajo el seno izquierdo.

Ve lo que has hecho de mí, la madre que devora a sus crías, la que se traga sus lágrimas y engorda, la que debe abortar en cada luna, la que sangra todos los días del año.

Así te he visto, vertiendo plomo derretido en las orejas inocentes, castrando bueyes, arrastrando tu azucena, tu inmaculado miembro, en la sangre de los mataderos. Disfrazado de mago o proxeneta en la plaza de la Bastilla—Jules te llamabas ese día y tus besos hedían a fósforo y cebolla.

De general en Bolivia, de tanquista en Vietnam, de eunuco en la puerta de los burdeles de la plaza México.

Formidable pelele frente al tablero de control; grand chef de la desgracia revolviendo catástrofes en la inmensa marmita celeste.

Ve lo que has hecho de mí.

Aquí estoy por tu mano en esta ineludible cámara de tortura, guiándome con sangre y con gemidos, ciega por obra y gracia de tu divina baba.

Mira mi piel de santa envejecida al paso de tu aliento, mira el tambor estéril de mi vientre que sólo conoce el ritmo de la anguistia, el golpe sordo de tu vientre que hace silbar al prisionero, al feto, a la mentira.

Valses y Otras Falsas Confesiones

WALTZ OF THE ANGELUS I

Look what you've made of me, the poorest saint in the
museum, the one in the last room, next to the johns, the
one with the black wound like an eye under the left temple.
Look what you've made of me, a mother who devours
her brood, who swallows her tears and gets fat,
who should abort with each moon, who bleeds
every day of the year.
I've seen you thus, spilling melted lead in
innocent ears, castrating bulls, dragging
lillies, your immaculate limb, in the slaughterhouse
blood. Disguised as a soothsayer or go-between
in Bastille plaza — you were called Jules
then and your kiss smelled of match and onion.
A general in Bolivia, a tank commander in Vietnam,
an eunuch in the brothels' door of the plaza Mexico.
A formidable strawman at the control panel;
The grand chef of adversity stirring catastrophes
in an immense celestial kettle.
Look what you've made of me.
By your hand I'm in this unavoidable torture
chamber, guided by blood and moans, blind
thanks to the labor and grace of your divine spit.
Look at my skin, that of an aged saint at your breath
rate, look at the sterile drum of my womb. It only
knows the rhythm of anguish, the mute thud of your
womb which makes the prisoner, the fetus, whistle
to the lie.

Translated by Nora Wieser
Valses y Otras Falsas Confesiones

VALS DEL ÁNGELUS II

Escucha las trompetas de tu reino. Noé naufraga
cada mañana, todo mar es terrible, todo sol es de
hielo, todo cielo es de piedra.
¿Qué más quieres de mí?
Quieres que ciega, irremediablemente a oscuras
deje de ser el alacrán en su nido, la tortuga de-
sollada, el árbol bajo el hacha, la serpiente sin
piel, el que vende a su madre con el primer vagi-
do, el que sólo es espalda y jamás frente, el que
siempre tropieza, el que nace de rodillas, el vipe-
rino, el potroso, el que enterró sus piernas y es-
tá vivo, el dueño de la otra mejilla, el que no sabe
amar como a sí mismo porque siempre está solo.
Ve lo que has hecho de mí. Predestinado estiér-
col, cieno de ojos vaciados.
Tu imagen en el espejo de la feria me habla de una
terrible semejanza.

Valses y Otras Falsas Confesiones

WALTZ OF THE ANGELUS II

Listen to the trumpets of your kingdom. Noah drowns
each morning, all the seas are terrible, all the suns
are ice, all the skies are stone.
What else do you want from me?
You want me blind, so that in darkness, I cease
irrevocably, to be the scorpion in its nest, the dead
turtle, the tree beneath the ax, the snake without its
skin, the one who sells his mother with the first cry,
the one who's only back and never front, the one who
always stumbles, the one who's born on his knees, the
spiteful man, the ruptured one, the one who buried his legs and
lives, the owner of the other cheek, the one who doesn't know how
to love as he loves himself, since he's always alone.
See what you've made of me.
Predestined dung, a mire with empty eyes.
Your image in the fun-house mirror speaks to me
of a terrible resemblance.

Translated by Nora Wieser
Valses y Otras Falsas Confesiones

Francisca Ossandón
Chile

FRANCISCA OSSANDON LIVES in Santiago but has traveled extensively. She is a youthful, vivacious woman who enjoys her circle of friends, delights in her new grandchild, jokes teasingly with her husband. And then there is her poetry. In an interview in a Chilean newspaper she implies two selves: "The self who responds to my poetry," she says, "is conditioned by violent and contradictory landscapes, and the people who inhabit them, and with the knowledge that we are obliged to receive fatalistically that which comes our way. On the other hand, in my way of being, I am my own person and I am happy because happiness is consubstantial to me and pleases me. I try to give and find it in my existence."

She is not interested in categories for her poetry. She is only concerned that it communicate feeling. Tangible or abstract as poetic labels are meaningless. She says: "Is a feeling which can become physical pain tangible or abstract? Is a premonition that, like a cloud, leaves everything in shadow, tangible or abstract?"

In her poetry one notes an absence of historical time. It is the voice of someone seeking to peel off layers of temporal circumstances in a search for the essential which might establish a validity for existence. The rhetorical questions are frequent. She says: "The past is like a book which I tend to leaf through rapidly while I smile with nostalgia, delight or sorrow, but I don't stay there. I don't know if I am only in the present or if I feel an urgency about the future." Perhaps it is this uncertainty which is reflected in her poetry as a lack of sequential, historical time.

Inevitably the poet is met with the reality of death. It is an interplay of shadows, a frequent theme, almost as a backdrop for much of her expression. There is nothing anecdotal in her style. At its best the reader is left with a sense of nobility, classic architectural form and timelessness in the manner of an ancient sage.

Books of Poetry

La Mano Abierta al Rayo	1957
Tiempo y Destiempo	1964
Diálogo Incesante	1971

V

Sombras revestidas de silencio
debilitan el verano
que dejo.
Arrebatan de la mirada
sus poblados núcleos.
De la boca, su simiente rebosante.
Alguien esconde
en tantas gotas heridas
la luz de las cosas terrenales,
y desnudos de claridad los días
van a tientas,
y otra es la dimensión de mis
noches.
Batida, yazgo con mis rodillas
alzadas,
las manos flojas en los sótanos
del destiempo.

Tiempo y Destiempo

V

Shadows dressed in silence
weaken the summer
I leave behind.
They steal inhabited centers
from my gaze.
Abundant seed
from my mouth.
In so many wounded drops
someone hides
the light of earthly things,
devoid of clarity, the days
feel their way along,
and my nights have another
dimension.
Exhausted, I lie with my knees
raised,
my hands slack in the cellars
of untime.

Translated by Nora Wieser
Tiempo y Destiempo

Despliegue de cortezas
por mi lengua
grabada como un tronco.
Busco la fuente
que enciende en mí
al cielo
devorado.
La validez de una
costumbre
transformada en agua
cenicienta.

Tiempo y Destiempo

The unfurling of bark
by my voice
etched like a tree's trunk.
I look for the source
which ignites in me
a devoured sky
The validity of a
custom
changed to
ashen water.

Translated by Nora Wieser
Tiempo y Destiempo

LOS JUEGOS DE LA TIERRA Y DE LA LUZ
I

Tierra.
De todo cuerpo su hondura.
Desnudo gesto.
En ella cien reflejos me afinan.
Lo que sabe y yo ignoro
es herida de toda edad.
Violenta tierra
que traduce en futuro
la nada.
Un día
me arrojará a los espacios
ahogada en su vacío,
los cabellos en temblor
como besos morados.

Sed.
Nueva sed, y tras la insaciada sed
un pájaro picotea
una doble palpitación acelerada.

Diálogo Incesante

GAMES OF EARTH AND LIGHT
I

Earth
Depth from all its body.
Naked gesture.
A hundred reflections tune me in.
What she knows and I ignore
is the wound of all the ages.
Violent earth
which translates the void
into future.
One day
I shall be hurled at the spaces,
drowned in the emptiness,
every hair trembling
like a bruised kiss.

Thirst.
New thirst, and behind the old
a bird pecks
at a doubly accelerated palpitation.

Translated by Nora Wieser
Diálogo Incesante

193

Olga Elena Mattei

OLGA ELENA MATTEI HAS LIVED most of her life in Colombia although she was born in 1933 in Puerto Rico. The poems selected for the anthology are from a book entitled *LA GENTE* published in 1974. The style and tone of this book is rather unique in Latin American women's poetry because it borders on the prosaic, and yet, enmasked in the colloquialisms, the wry humor, are the fundamental questions and concerns of a very contemporary being.

Besides the deadly accurate "conversations" of *La Gente,* her poetry includes a profound metaphysical expression such as the long prose poem "Pentafonía" written as five visions of humanity and the universe. This poem was adapted to music by the French composer Marc Carles and performed as a cantata in Paris in December, 1975. Besides the two works mentioned above she has published *Sílabas de Arena*, 1962 (Sand Syllables). In addition she has a number of unpublished volumes. Some of the poetry from these are included in *La Gente.*

In her introduction to *La Gente*, she writes with a sincerity characteristic of her poetry: "Around 1968 I found myself writing poems about people and things with a dry, austere tone . . . I hadn't yet read Nicanor Parra[1] and I asked myself if I had a right to call poetry, those prosaic

---

1. Nicanor Parra (1914–   ) is a Chilean poet who has gained considerable reknown for what he calls anti-poems. Parra says "the material I work with I find in everyday life."

194

bits of my daily living . . . But I couldn't do more than obey an internal and unconscious thermometer.

The climax was a poem I wrote about the hinge . . . I'm moved by its simplicity, its functionality, the ingeniousness of its invention, its longevity, after centuries of man's history, the miracle of its effect. But it was too much to pretend, on saying this, that the reader would capture its poetic quality and all of that would succeed in moving the reader in the same way . . . With these thoughts I was preoccupied about the validity of contemporary art, during a long and detailed trip of more than six months visiting museums and archeological sites in Europe and the Middle East, immersed in the extraordinary values of ancient art. My world of criteria was coming apart, when, one day, thinking about my poem on the hinge, I entered a giant room of the Museum of Modern Art in Amsterdam . . . and suddenly, facing me, placed on an important wall . . . a gigantic, shining hinge! Another artist had thought and felt the same as I! I wasn't so crazy after all!"

Books of Poetry

Sílabas de Arena	1962
Pentafonía	1964
La Gente	1974

195

Yo soy una señora burguesa
con la barriga inflada
y escribo poesías
con dolor de garganta.
He sido
niña prodigio
muchachita insoportable
mala estudiante
reina de belleza
modelo
de esas que anuncian
sopas, o telas o artículos diversos . . .
me metí en este lío
inevitable
de enamorarme
y sacrificar a un pobre hombre
hasta convertirlo en un marido
(sin mencionar de paso
en qué
me he convertido)
y cometí el abuso social
imperdonable
de tener cinco hijos.
He fracasado como madre
como esposa
como amante
como lectora
como filósofa.
Lo único que puedo hacer
mediocremente bien
es ser
señora
burguesa y despreciable,
imperdonablemente inútil.
Y eso
es precisamente lo que me infla

I am a bourgeois wife
with a swollen belly
and I write poems
with a sore throat.
I've been
an intolerable child
bad student
beauty queen
a model
one of those that advertise
soups or cloth or sundries . . .
I got myself into this inevitable mess
of falling in love
and sacrificing one poor man
until I converted him into a husband
(without mentioning in passing
what
I have become)
and I committed the unforgiveable
social abuse of
having five children.
I have failed as a mother
wife
lover
reader
philosopher,
All that I can do mediocrely well
is be
a lady
bourgeois and despicable,
unforgiveably useless.
And that
is precisely what has swollen

la barriga
y me hace escribir poesías
con el dolor de garganta
que me saca la rabia.
Porque todos los días me acuerdo
de la guerra y el hambre
que son tan reales como las señoras
a la misma hora
en que yo estoy aquí sentada
como una pendeja.

La Gente

my belly
and with a sore throat
makes me write the poetry
that lets out my anger.
Because every day I remember
the war and the hunger,
as real as bourgeois ladies
at the same time
that I sit here
like a dumbbell.

Translated by Priscilla Joslin
La Gente

¿Recuerdas,
tu cara entre la sopa,
y aquella náusea
que daba la zanahoria?
Y metérsela a la boca,
y vomitarla . . .
y tener hoy todavía
la misma cara de ese día,
cerrar los ojos y sentirla,
como si fuera ahora,
untada toda en babas y lágrimas,
cuatro años uno haciéndose persona,
y no querer la zanahoria
pero de todos modos,
esforzarse en tragarla,
con esa gente atrás
que tiene la intención de educar
vigilando firmemente
y uno sí quiere complacerles,
pero la vuelve a vomitar . . .
Y uno no aprende a comer zanahoria,
pero años después,
descubre que cuando uno estuvo
esos años "haciéndose persona,"
sí aprendió al fin a "tragarse"
de algún modo
cualquier cosa.

La Gente

Do you remember,
your face in the soup,
and that nausea
brought on by carrots?
And putting them in your mouth,
and vomiting them . . .
You still have that same face today,
close your eyes and feel it happen
as though it were now,
smeared with drool and tears
four years becoming a person
and not liking carrots
but forcing yourself to swallow them
anyway,
with those people behind you
intent on educating
guarding rigidly,
you wanting to please them,
but vomiting again . . .
and you never learned to eat carrots;
years later you
discover that in all that time
spent "becoming a person"
you did learn, finally, to "swallow"
almost everything
somehow.

                    Translated by Priscilla Joslin
                    La Gente

Diciembre treinta y uno
de mil novecientos cualquier cosa.
¿Y qué me importa?
Treinta y uno de diciembre
y estoy sola
y pienso en los repartidores de Coca-Cola
trabajando
a última hora
al calor de este cielo
depresivamente bello
y ajeno.
Verano para los que saben aprovecharlo.
Fin de año
para los que fueron buenos
y prometen
ser felices el próximo año.
En casa
ya nada celebramos.
-"Juana, vaya dígales
a los hombres de la Coca-Cola
que los amo
y les deseo
Feliz Año
Nuevo.
Dígales también que les regalo
la piscina del vecino,
el sueldo del marido,
mi anillo,
mi carro."
-"¡Usted parece loca!
y además
ellos
ya se fueron,
señora."

La Gente

December thirty first
nineteen hundred anything
and what does it matter?
December thirty first
and I'm alone
and I think of the Coca-Cola deliverymen
working
at the last minute
in the heat of this sky
depressingly beautiful
and foreign.
Summer for those who know how to enjoy it.
Year's end
for those who were good
and promise
to be happy next year.
At home
we no longer celebrate.
-"Juana, go tell
the Coca-Cola men
that I love them
and I wish them
a happy
New Year.
Tell them also that I'm giving them
the neighbor's pool,
my husband's salary,
my ring,
my car."
-"You sound crazy,
and besides
they've already left
ma'am."

Translated by Priscilla Joslin
La Gente

Las galletas de soda
pareadas
se parten
por cualquier parte,
menos por la parte
perforada
para que se partan.
Las parejas,
quiero decir,
las personas,
todas,
digo, las cosas,
perdón, me refiero a las galletas,
ustedes saben,
se parten
por . . .

La Gente

Pairs
of soda crackers
part
anywhere,
but along the perforation
The pairs, couples
I mean,
the people,
all
I mean, things,
pardon, I'm referring to the crackers,
you know,
they part
along . . .

Translated by Priscilla Joslin
La Gente

Yo soy aquí
sentada en este sitio
siempre, o casi siempre
o tendida aquí mismo,
con los pies hacia el este
y este creer
que soy así.
Ni un solo día me dispongo
cabeza al sur
o pies arriba,
no doy vuelta a la cama
diariamente,
y me amoldan los muebles
con su estafa
de funcionalidad.
Las cosas que poseo
me poseen
y me gasto la vida
en ordenarlas,
asearlas, restaurarlas,
soportarlas,
muy rara vez en disfrutarlas
verdaderamente.

Si acaso entre el tiempo se resbalan
diez minutos de pausa
para escarbar en las palabras
que los libros me guardan,
los gasto irrevocablemente
en despegar el polvo de las tapas
y abrir el ficho clasifista
que me impuso en el sistema
esta eficiente y progresista tecnocracia.
Pero volviendo al tema de la cama,
quisiera que un día me encontraran
el marido, los hijos, los parientes,

I am here
seated in this place
always, or almost always
or stretched out right here,
with my feet to the east
and the belief
that I am this way.
Not even one day
does my head point south
or my feet up
I don't turn the bed
daily,
and my furniture molds me
with its deceit
of functionalism.
The things I own
own me
and I spend my life
arranging them in order,
putting up with them,
rarely enjoying them
really.

If maybe in amongst time
ten minutes of pause slip by
where I can dig into the words
which books hold for me,
I waste them irrevocably
brushing dust from the tops
and opening the classifying file
by which this efficient and progressive technocracy
placed me in the system.
But getting back to the theme of the bed,
I'd like one day for
the husband, the children, the relatives,

debajo del colchón,
o simplemente,
con la cama hacia el norte,
en mitad de la sala.
Malditas las casillas
con que nos clasifican
las espaldas,
y los computadores racionales
que programan dentro de mi cerebro
mi propia idiosincrasia,
imponiéndole horarios a la vida
y fechas a la luz de la mañana.

La Gente

to find me under the mattress
or simply in the middle of the room
with the bed facing north.
Damn the stereotypes
by which we are cast,
and the rational computers
that program my own idiosyncracy inside my brain,
imposing timetables on life
and dates on the morning light.

Translated by Priscilla Joslin
La Gente

Nancy Bacelo
Uruguay
1933–

IN URUGUAY, Nancy Bacelo is extremely well known not only for her poetry but for her many other activities as well. She is a woman of amazing energies. In 1960 she inaugurated and organized the National Book Fair of Uruguay which she still directs. It is a thirty day exposition of books, : nd fine handcrafts. It includes free concerts, films, dance, and theatre, attracting vast crowds. In addition she directs the expositions of an art gallery which is at the open end of a shopping mall. Her creativity results in unusual arrangements of exhibits. One vivid example: weavings on translucent, multihued panels suspended from the ceiling and mounds of watermelons in clusters on the floor. In accord with her credo of the need for art to be accessible, she has arranged a table and benches of Scandinavian design directly in the middle of the gallery. The daily newspapers, surrounded by the wonderful exhibits, are on the table free for reading by the mall shoppers. With her unique talents, Nancy has been a prime force in recent Uruguayan cultural history.

In her poetry she speaks of living without self betrayal, not evading what life has to offer, even though there is pain, the pain of memories, or of the present. Yet, the future does not equate despair. Among her poems one does find the positive notes of faith in human potential and a better time in the future. Some of her prevalent themes are found in her popular book of ballads, CANTARES, which first appeared in 1960. She believes unequivocally in poetry which comes, as she says "from the heart." She rejects the poetry of a "laboratory." Contrived poetry, she feels, is too easily detected.

Books of Poetry

Tránsito de Fuego	1956
Círculo Nocturno	1959
Cantares	1960
Cielo Solo	1962
Razón de la Existencia	1964
Barajando	1967
Las Pruebas de la Suerte	1969
El Pan de Cada Día	1975
Las Coplas de Nico Pérez	1978

No me interesan los datos
los precisos datos de las cosas
No me interesan los relojes
Que no son de sol
Ni la lista
de los amores que se van
Me interesa eso sí la verdad
El ruido del mar
las horas que se pasan
la luz sobre la cama al mediodía
y todo lo que viene
y se va
sin nombre y sin aviso
sucediéndose
como las cosas sencillas
se suceden

I'm not interested in facts
precise facts of things
I'm not interested in clocks
unless their origin is the sun
Nor lists
of loves that have ended
I'm most interested in
the sound of the sea
the hours that pass
Sunrays on the bed at mid-day
and everything that comes and goes
without name or notice
following one after the other
as simple things do

Translated by Nora Wieser

MUY BAJITO

Los ritmos ciertos
cuando la casa se silencia
y ha quedado el mantel
y conversamos
"-Europa está tan lejos-
los amigos se han ido
hubo noticias de Cristina
y de Ida y del Gordo
están arrancando los plátanos
en dieciocho de julio"
hay como una niebla que no pasa
mientras flamean las banderas
y hubo tres grados bajo cero
sobre los huesos de los obstinados
en seguir con los pies sobre esta tierra.

El Pan de Cada Día

IN A VERY, VERY QUIET VOICE

The familiar rhythms
when the house goes quiet
and the tablecloth stays
and we talk
"—Europe is so far away—
our friends have gone
news from Cristina
and Ida and Gordo
they're uprooting plane-trees
on the 18th of July Ave."
There's something like a fog which doesn't end,
while the flags wave
and it was three below zero
in the bones of those obstinate
enough to persist with their
feet on this land.

Translated by Nora Wieser
El Pan de Cada Día

De vos de mí teñidos habitantes
claritos como el agua de esta copa
de vos de mí de vida tal de muerte
vestidos con el lujo de esta ropa
se probarán los trajes los que saben
se teñirán las bocas los que pueden
desnudarán sus cuerpos los que entienden
que ya no hay tiempo que perder
que llaman y no hay tiempo que perder
que voltean y no hay tiempo que perder
que nos toman el pulso
que nos miden
que nos reclaman la conciencia
y no hay tiempo
no hay tiempo más tiempo que perder.

El Pan de Cada Día

From you from me painted dwellers
transparent as the water in this cup
from you from me from life like death
dressed with the luxury of these garments
those who know will try the clothes on
those who can will paint their mouths
they will bare their bodies, those who understand
there is no more time to lose
they call and there is no time to lose
they turn and there is no time to lose
they take our pulse
they measure us
they demand our conscience
and there is no time
no time more time to lose.

Translated by Nora Wieser
El Pan de Cada Día

Me sorprendo en lugares
donde nunca estuviera
por ejemplo en este
café lejano y solo
sobre una mesa oscura
y desteñida
me sorprendo llamándote
diciéndote
que ese tango que suena
y dice "corazón no le hagas caso"
ese tango ˙
sonando en medio de la lluvia
que querés
me deshace

El Pan de Cada Día

I surprise myself in places
where I would never be
for example in this
café remote and lonely
at a dark, faded table
I surprise myself calling out to you
telling you
that the tango playing
saying "never mind my heart"
that tango
sounding in the middle of the rain
what do you expect
it destroys me.

Translated by Nora Wieser
El Pan de Cada Día

TODAVÍA ES TEMPRANO

Son las secuencias de amor imaginado
los por si acaso
cuando la luz se expande
esas reservas que cada uno guarda
con la esperanza
de volverlas ciertas.
Pero meras palabras corregidas
resultan a la noche.
Vuelan gaviotas en el cielo claro
Para cortar las alas bastaría
desparramar el sueño
y hoy no es mañana todavía.

El Pan de Cada Día

IT'S STILL EARLY

They are the sequences of an imagined love
the "in cases"
when the light expands
the reserves everyone holds
with the illusion
of making them reality.
But in the night they become
mere words corrected.
Seagulls fly in a clear sky.
To cut their wings one need only
squander the illusions
and today isn't yet tomorrow.

Translated by Nora Wieser
El Pan de Cada Día

Belkis Cuza Malé

Cuba
1942–

BIRTH

On a 15th day
they gave me a name.
A Name
with desperate letters
that my father found
spewed out
on the tired crossword page
of his troubles.

I was born in the month of June
in the middle of his sadness.
It was night time
when I entered my house . . .

THE POEM "Birth" is from Belkis Cuza Male's first book *Viento en La Pared* (Wind on the Wall). She was then nineteen years old, a girl from Santiago de Cuba in virtual literary isolation. She started writing poetry at fifteen and remembers submitting a collection of poems to a women's magazine, all carefully hand copied and illustrated with her own drawings. The woman editor wrote a letter which began: "Belkis, you will never become a poet . . ."

Her first two books won an honorable mention in the esteemed Casa de Las Americans literary competition and she was able to leave Santiago's isolation and go to Havana where she came in contact with other poets and writers. She met her husband, Heberto Padilla, another fine Cuban poet, at this time. Belkis Cuza Malé belongs to the generation of young writers who received recognition during the early years of the Revolution.

There is a definite evolution from her first book to the book *Juego de Damas* (Ladies' Game).[1] *Viento en la Pared* (Wind on the Wall) is a

---

1. Juego de Damas is also the name for the game of checkers.

222

book that describes a tender, sensitive awakening to the poet's self and to the world around her. There is a magical wistfulness in the images. They are delicate—so fragile it seems they might shatter if one turns the page abruptly. *Juego de Damas*, on the other hand, has an outspoken, often irreverent tone. Many of the poems are portraits, particularly portraits of women whose condition as women the poet has observed or reflected upon. She sees a mutual dependency in the relationship of men and women. Yet she feels this mutuality is not always recognized by men. Also, women, she feels, are often not internally liberated sufficiently to define in a positive way their position in their society. She does not see a parallel between racial and sexual prejudices. She feels the former are more easily eliminated. A woman, she says, is biologically bound—she feels a more profound responsibility for the raising of children. It is an innate preoccupation in women which conditions their entire lives, if they have children.

Sometimes, she feels the need to be able to devote all her time to writing. On the other hand, her duties in her community, as a wife, mother, homemaker, provide her with a sense of participation in life, that she feels is essential for the intellectual. A writer, she feels, should not remain cold and aloof from the society.[2]

Integration or better, the lack of it, is a frequent theme in *Juego de Damas* as evidenced by poems like "Faust," or "The Shrew Who Married God." The forceful use of irony in the book resembles other contemporary women's poetry, Rosario Castellanos, Anne Sexton, Adrienne Rich —perhaps it forms part of a historical process in the unveiling of women's expression in literature.

Books of Poetry

El Viento en la Pared	1962
Tiempos de Sol	1963
Los Alucinados	1963
Cartas a Ana Frank	1966
Juego de Damas (unpublished manuscript)	

---

2. These observations were made in an interview with the editor in Havana, August 25, 1978.

LOS FOTOGÉNICOS

Por las esquinas amarillentas de la hoja de papel,
se les ve caminar, desaparecer al doblar la página.
Habitan una isla en el trópico de la guerra,
una isla donde todos los vasos están rotos,
una isla a caballo.
Entran en los suburbios de la tarde
y en los hoteles de paso,
navegan en una cama de velas blancas,
mientras él canta y ella es un ruido más,
una ola debajo de la cama.
Mejor callarse y dejarlos que duerman
              y dejarlos que vivan
              y dejarlos que mueran.
Al pie de la foto unas cuantas líneas
atestiguan el hecho:
ninguno está seguro del otro,
pero navegan,
navegan con la isla por todos los mares del mundo.

Juego de Damas

THE PHOTOGENIC ONES

You see them walking along the yellowed corners of the album,
disappearing as you turn the page.
They inhabit an island in the war zone,
with all the glasses shattered,
an island on horseback.
They enter the suburbs of the afternoon
and the hotels by the wayside,
navigating on a bed of white sails
while he sings and she is one more noise,
a wave beneath the bed.
Quiet now, let them sleep
        live
        die.
A few lines at the bottom of the photo
witness the fact:
that neither is sure of the other
but they sail,
sail with the island on all the seas of the world.

Translated by Nora Wieser
Juego de Damas

LAS CENICIENTAS

Somos las cenicientas.
El señor Botticelli pintó para nosotras
las tres hadas madrinas.
No somos inocentes.
El Príncipe nunca nos ha besado.
No hemos pisado su recámara,
ni lamido su vientre.
Vivimos en la cocina,
nuestra luna es el fuego.
Nuestros pies son enormes;
un largo baño no nos vendría mal.
Andamos con sayas rotas,
con las greñas al aire
y comemos pan duro.
No somos inocentes.
Por negritas, por feas y por putas
fuimos chifladas en el certamen de Miss Universo.
Pero gritamos (las deslenguadas)
¡merde! al culo del rey
y ¡merde! a sus ministros,
aunque ellos rabien con nuestra peste.

Juego de Damas

THE STEPSISTERS

We are the stepsisters.
Mr. Botticelli painted
three fairy godmothers for us.
We're not innocents.
The Prince never kissed us.
We've never set foot in his bedroom
or licked his belly.
We live in the kitchen,
our moon is the fire.
Our feet are enormous;
we could do with a bath.
Our dresses are tattered,
hair like a mop in the wind,
eating day-old bread.
We're not innocents.
Being dark, ugly, promiscuous
they booed us at the Miss Universe pageant
But we screamed (foulmouthed)
¡merde! to the kind's arse
and ¡merde! to his ministers.
even though they rage with our pest.

Translated by Nora Wieser
Juego de Damas

227

OH, MI RIMBAUD

He aquí que Rimbaud y yo nos hacemos al mar
en un gran elefante blanco,
nos perdemos en la bruma inconsolable de unos ojos
y como colegiales reincidimos de pronto
en el amor.
El me toma la mano y la rechazo con un grito.
Luego,
se abandona a las aguas
y atraviesa otros mares y otros ojos
y se queda sin mí,
me regala la cabellera roja de sus sueños,
el pálido color de sus mejillas,
un espejo.

Cuando aminore la tormenta y su caballo
descubra el camino,
volverá dueño y señor del vellocino de oro,
jovial y para entonces harto ya de mí.

Juego de Damas

OH, MY RIMBAUD

And so Rimbaud and I set out to sea
on a great white elephant,
lost in a mist of destiny with our eyes.
Like school kids we fall in love again.
He takes my hand, I pull away with a shout.
Then,
He gives in to the waters
and crosses other seas, other eyes
without me,
leaving as a gift the shock of red hair from his dreams,
the pale color of his cheeks,
a mirror.

When the storm dies down and his horse
finds the way,
he'll return as Lord and Master of the Golden Fleece,
in high spirits and by that time,
sick of me.

Translated by Nora Wieser
Juego de Damas

MUJER BRAVA QUE CASÓ CON DIOS
A Sor Juana Ines de la Cruz

Me la imagino toda de blanco
pintando las paredes del convento con malas palabras,
abrumada por el calor, por los mosquitos
y el desierto que era su celda.
Supongo que mucho antes, había cometido un desliz
con un caballero que por aquel tiempo
ya era casado, pero que reconstruía su vida de soltero
cada vez que la besaba.
Estoy segura de que cuando él la abandonó
ella quiso entregar su cuerpo al diablo,
hacerse una mujer práctica e indigna
y que compró dos o tres trapos femeninos,
lloró un poco
y luego se dijo: "toda la maldad del mundo son los hombres."
Creo, es más,
que no procuró olvidarlo,
que llevó un record de las batallas que ganaba
y que solamente cuando lo mataron
en aquel lío de mujeres
ella puso sus ojos en otro
y que casó con Dios, el impotente.

Juego de Damas

THE SHREW WHO MARRIED GOD
To Sor Juana Inez de la Cruz

I imagine her all in white
painting the convent walls with dirty words,
overcome by the heat, the mosquitos,
the desert of her cell.
Much earlier, I imagine, she committed an impropriety
with a married gentleman
who became a bachelor again,
each time he kissed her.
I'm certain that when he abandoned her,
she wanted to surrender her body to the devil,
become a practical, indignant woman,
and she bought two or three feminine things,
cried a bit
and then said: "All the world's evil is men."
I believe, moreover,
that she never tried to forget that.
She kept a record of battles won
and only when they killed him
in a maze of other women,
did she turn her eyes toward another
and she married God, the impotent one.

Translated by Nora Wieser
Juego de Damas

FAUSTO

Cuidado con ese hombre que atraviesa la puerta.
Puede ser Fausto.
En sus manos hay huellas de vejez. El modo
        con que lleva a los labios el cigarro
dice que ha andado mucho por el mundo.
Observen el libidinoso ojo derecho, el único
        que salvó de la metralla. La frente estirada
como un guante, sus ropas compradas
en tiendas exclusivas de París.

Cuando todos duermen, cuando el único ruido
en la calle es el carrito del basurero o el grito
        del sonámbulo, apura la copa
de vino rojo;
por un instante su rostro se transforma y brilla
        como un pez en las profundidades.
¿Quién le ha dado el secreto? ¿Es que otros Faustos
recorren la ciudad?

Muy temprano hace gimnasia frente al espejo enorme
                                del baño.
Nadie lo observa, nadie sabe que a solas baila la suiza,
improvisa una pelea con su doble hasta que el otro cae
jadeante o noqueado por su puño.
¿Quién no lo ha visto recorriendo la ciudad
en su VW, firmando órdenes de compra o viviendo
con la moral de la época?
Pero no fue el amor lo que hizo de este hombre
                lo que es hoy.
Las Margaritas tenían ya su misma edad
y vivían de aparatosas costumbres.
Fausto no se interesó nunca por ellas,
no se enamoró locamente de ninguna.

Juego de Damas

FAUST

Watch out for that man coming in the door.
He may be Faust.
Traces of age on his hands. The way
       he brings the cigar to his lips —
he's seen a lot of the world.
Observe the lecherous right eye, the only one
      saved from the shrapnel. His forehead stretched
like a glove, his clothes
from exclusive Paris shops.

When everyone's sleeping, when the only noise
on the street is the trashcart or a sleepwalker's shout,
      he empties his glass of red wine;
for a moment his face shines
like a fish in the ocean depths.
Who has given him the secret? Are other Fausts
running around the city?

He does exercises in front of the huge bathroom mirror.
No one sees him, no one knows he waltzes alone,
improvises a boxing match with his double whom he
knocks to the floor with his punch.
Has anyone not seen him around the city in his VW, signing
purchase orders or living
the morals of the time?

But it wasn't love that made him this way.
Those Marguerites were his same age,
existing among pretentious customs.
Faust was never interested in them,
he never fell crazy in love with anyone.

Translated by Nora Wiser
Juego de Damas

ESTÁN HACIENDO UNA MUCHACHA PARA LA EPOCA

Están haciendo una muchacha para la época,
con mucha cal y unas pocas herramientas,
alambres, cabelleras postizas,
senos de algodón y armazón de madera.
El rostro tendrá la inocencia de Ofelia
y las manos, el rito de una Helena de Troya.
Hablará tres idiomas
y será diestra en el arco, en el tiro y la flecha.
Están haciendo una muchacha para la época,
entendida en política
y casi en filosofía,
alguien que no tartamudee,
ni tenga necesidad de espejuelos,
que llene los requisitos de una aeromoza,
lea a diario la prensa
y, por supuesto, libere su sexo
sin dar un mal paso con un hombre.

En fin, si no hay nuevas disposiciones,
así saldrá del horno
esta muchacha hecha para la época.

Juego de Damas

THEY'RE MAKING A GIRL FOR THE AGE

They're making a girl for the times,
with a lot of lime, a few tools,
wires, wigs, cotton breasts and a wooden shell.
Her face will have Ophelia's innocence
her hands the ritual of a Helen of Troy.
She'll speak three languages,
be adept at archery, shooting, and arrows.
They're making a girl for the age.
She'll understand politics
and philosophy, almost,
someone who doesn't stutter,
need glasses,
looks like an airline stewardess,
reads the papers every day
and, of course, frees her sex
without tripping any males.

In the end, if there are no new requirements,
that's the way she'll come out of the oven,
this girl made for the age.

Translated by Nora Wieser
Juego de Damas

235

Alejandra Pizarnik
Argentina
1936–1972

ALEJANDRA PIZARNIK WAS BORN in 1936 in Buenos Aires. She studied philosophy and letters at the University of Buenos Aires. She then studied painting under Juan Batlle Planas. In the early 1960's she was in Paris where she began to contribute both criticism and poetry to various French and Spanish periodicals. She also translated into Spanish French poets such as Antonin Artaud, Henri Michaux and Aimé Césaire.

Her own poetry is described in the words of her friend, André Pierre de Mandiargues, who wrote to her saying: "I frequently reread your poems and I give them to others to read and I feel love for them. They are beautiful animals, a bit cruel, a bit neurasthenic and sensitive; they are most beautiful animals: one has to nurture and fondle them; they are precious small furies covered with fur, perhaps a type of chinchilla: one has to pet them and give them luxurious blood."[1]

As Pizarnik speaks of her own poetry we find the personality carefully interwoven with the conscience of the artist: "Each day my poems are more brief: small flames for the someone who was lost in a strange world. In a few lines I find the eyes of someone I know waiting, I find reconciled things, hostile things, things that the unknown never ceases to contribute; and my eternal thirst, my hunger, my horror . . . I believe orthodoxically in inspiration, but it doesn't prevent me, entirely the contrary, from concentrating a good deal of time on one poem. And I do it in such a way that one is reminded perhaps, of the gesture of the plastic artists: I fasten the page to the wall and I contemplate it; I change words, I cross out lines. Sometimes on crossing out one word, I imagine another one in

---

1. Cristina Peri Rossi, "Alejandra Pizarnik o la tentación de la muerte," *Cuadernos Hispanoamericanos*, vol. 273, (1973): 584-588.

its place, but without yet knowing its name. Then, while waiting for the one I want, I make a drawing in the empty place which alludes to the word. And that drawing is like a ritual of calling."[2]

Cristina Peri Rossi, an Uruguayan poet, synthesizes Pizarnik's world by saying: "the poetry of Pizarnik moved between the horror of sterility (that "silence" so much feared in her writings), the lack of confidence regarding the possibilities of communication with language, a fear of insanity (which is the extreme of incommunicability), and the presentiment of death."[3] In regard to the latter, one must add that her poetry indicates more than presentiment. Often it seems to anguish in a *living* death. The tension of her language is like a series of shocks that the reader undergoes, being somehow, fast in the grip of the words. Cristina Peri Rossi observes that "almost everything in the poetry of Alejandra Pizarnik seemed to be announcing that ritual gesture which would lead her, two weeks before Ezra Pound's death, to commit suicide alone in Buenos Aires."[4]

Books of Poetry

La Tierra Más Ajena	1955
La Última Inocencia	1956
Las Aventuras Perdidas	1958
Árbol de Diana	1962
Los Trabajos y las Noches	1965
Extracción de la Piedra de la Locura	1968
Nombres y Figuras	1969
El Infierno Musical	1971

---

2. Cesar Magrini, ed., *Quince Poetas* (Buenos Aires: Centurion, 1963).
3. Peri Rossi, p. 585.
4. *Ibid.*, p. 587.

237

PIDO EL SILENCIO

                    canta, lastimada mía
                    Cervantes

aunque es tarde, es noche,
y tú no puedes.

Canta como si no pasara nada.

Nada pasa.

                    Los Trabajos y las Noches

238

I ASK SILENCE
> sing, my pain
> Cervantes

although it is late, it's night,
and you can't.

Sing as if nothing were happening.

Nothing is happening.

Translated by Susan Pensak
Los Trabajos y las Noches

ANTES

a Eva Durrell

bosque musical

los pájaros dibujaban en mis ojos
pequeñas jaulas

Los Trabajos y las Noches

BEFORE
to Eva Durrel

musical forest

in my eyes the birds used to sketch
small cages

Translated by Susan Pensak
Los Trabajos y las Noches

MORADAS

a Théodore Fraenkel

En la mano crispada de un muerto,
en la memoria de un loco,
en la tristeza de un niño,
en la mano que busca el vaso,
en el vaso inalcanzable,
en la sed de siempre.

Los Trabajos y las Noches

ABODES
to Théodore Fraenkel

In the spastic hand of a corpse,
in the memory of a madman,
in the sorrow of a child,
in the hand that seeks the glass,
in the glass that can't be reached,
in the thirst of always.

Translated by Susan Pensak
Los Trabajos y las Noches

AMANTES

una flor
          no lejos de la noche
          mi cuerpo mudo
      se abre
a la delicada urgencia del rocío

Los Trabajos y las Noches

244

LOVERS

a blossom
        not far from night
      my mute body
   opens
to the delicate urgency of the dew

Translated by Susan Pensak
Los Trabajos y las Noches

VERDE PARAISO

extraña que fuí
cuando vecina de lejanas luces
atesoraba palabras muy puras
para crear nuevos silencios

Los Trabajos y las Noches

GREEN PARADISE

I was strange
as a neighbor of distant lights
hoarding very pure words
in order to create new silences

Translated by Susan Pensak
Los Trabajos y las Noches

CREPÚSCULO

La sombra cubre pétalos mirados
El viento lleva el último gesto de una hoja
El mar ajeno y doblemente mudo
en el verano que apiada por sus luces

Un deseo aquí
Una memoria de allá

Los Trabajos y las Noches

DUSK

The dark covers watched petals
The wind lifts the last semblance of a leaf
The sea remote and doubly mute
in the summer that evokes pity for its lights

A longing from here
A memory from there

Translated by Susan Pensak
Los Trabajos y las Noches

NOMBRARTE

No el poema de tu ausencia,
sólo un dibujo, una grieta en un muro,
algo en el viento, un sabor amargo.

Los Trabajos y las Noches

TO NAME YOU

Not the poem of your absence,
only a drawing, a crack in a wall,
something in the wind, a bitter taste.

Translated by Susan Pensak
Los Trabajos y las Noches

LAS GRANDES PALABRAS

a Antonio Porchia

aún no es ahora
ahora es nunca

aún no es ahora
ahora y siempre
es nunca

Los Trabajos y las Noches

THE GREAT WORDS
to Antonio Porchia

even though it is not now
now is never

even though it is not now
now and forever
is never

Translated by Susan Pensak
Los Trabajos y las Noches

FRONTERAS INÚTILES

un lugar
no digo un espacio
hablo de
        qué
hablo de lo que no es
hablo de lo que conozco

no el tiempo
sólo todos los instantes
no el amor
no
    sí
no

un lugar de ausencia
un hilo de miserable unión

Los Trabajos y las Noches

USELESS FRONTIERS

a place
I do not say a space
I speak of
           what
I speak of what is not
I speak of what I know

not time
just all the moments
not love
no
    yes
no

a place of absence
a thread of miserable union

Translated by Susan Pensak
Los Trabajos y las Noches

RELOJ

Dama pequeñísima
moradora en el corazón de un pájaro
sale al alba a pronunciar una sílaba
NO

Los Trabajos y las Noches

CLOCK

Tiny lady
dweller in the heart of a bird
goes out at daybreak to pronounce one syllable
NO

Translated by Susan Pensak
Los Trabajos y las Noches

FIESTA

He desplegado mi orfandad
sobre la mesa, como un mapa.
Dibujé el itinerario
hacia mi lugar al viento.
Los que llegan no me encuentran.
Los que espero no existen.

Y he bebido licores furiosos
para transmutar los rostros
en un ángel, en vasos vacíos.

Los Trabajos y las Noches

258

PARTY

I've unrolled my orphan's legacy
on the table, like a map.
I drew directions
toward my place in the wind
Those who come don't find me.
Those I wait for don't exist.

And I've drunk violent liquors
to transmute the faces
into an angel, into empty glasses.

Translated by Susan Pensak
Los Trabajos y las Noches

259

SORTILEGIOS

Y las damas vestidas de rojo para mi dolor y con mi
dolor insumidas en mi soplo, agazapadas como fetos de
escorpiones en el lado más interno de mi nuca, las
madres de rojo que me aspiran el único calor que me
doy con mi corazón que apenas pudo nunca latir, a mí
que siempre tuve que aprender sola cómo se hace para
beber y comer y respirar y a mí que nadie me enseñó a
llorar y nadie me enseñará ni siquiera las grandes
damas adheridas a la entretela de mi respiración con
babas rojizas y velos flotantes de sangre, mi sangre,
la mía sola, la que yo me procuré y ahora vienen a
beber de mí haber matado al rey que flota en
el río y mueve los ojos y sonríe pero está muerto y
cuando alguien está muerto, muerto está por más que
sonría y las grandes, las trágicas damas de rojo han
matado al que se va río abajo y yo me quedo como rehén
en perpetua posesión.

Extracción de la Piedra de Locura

SORCERIES

And the ladies dressed in red for my pain and with
my pain unsinking in my breath, crouched like scorpions'
fetuses in the innermost nape of the neck, the mothers
in red who want to take from me the only warmth I give
myself with my heart which could hardly ever beat, from
me who always had to learn alone what one does in order
to drink and eat and breathe and from me whom no one ever
taught to cry and no one will teach me not even the great
ladies stuck to the lining of my breathing with reddish
spit and floating veils of blood, my blood, mine alone
that I got myself and now they come to drink of me after
having just killed the king who floats in the river and
moves his eyes and smiles but he is dead and when some-
one is dead, he's dead no matter how much he smiles and
the great ones, the tragic ladies in red have killed him
who goes down river and I remain like a hostage in per-
petual possession.

Translated by Susan Pensak
Extracción de la Piedra de Locura

Cristina Meneghetti
Uruguay
1948–

QUIET, EVEN TIMID, Cristina Meneghetti has a lithe, dancer's body and enormous blue eyes which openly reveal a great sensitivity. Even after a brief meeting one is impressed by her intelligence. She speaks French and Italian fluently and has translated into Spanish, contemporary Italian poets. Her own poetry has a major work called *Juego Abierto*, (Open Play). The book is divided into three parts; first: "how to straighten the mess," a series of poems which deal with self-identity. The second part, "leave everything and listen to me," is the poet's expression of love, both as a painful and fulfilling experience. The third part of the book, entitled "clarity corrected" is protest poetry expansive and profound enough not to be limited to historical circumstances.

One of her most effective techniques is the use of prosaic experiences or language to articulate a great anguish. She then creates an effective tension because of the contrast between the mundane and the underlying depth of feeling. The poem "I need you . . ." is an excellent example of this technique. The ending of this poem leaves the reader shaken. We expect something more in keeping with the prosaic language of the rest of the poem. Yet there is a quiet urgency in the tone which is revealed through the imperative and also through a kind of slow pulsating rhythm the language creates.

She talks about the process of writing in the following unpublished
poem:

> soliloquy of three this
> mute dialogue
> of paper pencil person
> dynamiting ourselves patiently
> in the vain effort
> of a pirate with no treasure.

"Dynamiting . . . patiently" seems an accurate description of her poetry's
impact on the reader. Her view of people's destiny is essentially fatalistic.
Her poetry often sees a human as a frightened, vulnerable being involved
in a futile search for meaning in existence. To portray "this poor skeleton"
as she says in one of her poems, she uses carefully chosen language with
a precise, steady rhythm and no violent crescendos.

Books of Poetry

Intento	1968
Juego Abierto	1972
Tiempo Fiero	1976

la forma de dar forma al pensamiento
de ir poniendo cada pedacito
en su lugar
cada conexión en su punto
no fuera
que pasara algo imprevisto
y no se tuviera la respuesta
pronta.

Juego Abierto

the utter form of giving form to thought
of going along putting each little piece
in its place
each connection to its point
in case something unforeseen should happen
and one wouldn't have a ready
answer.

Translated by Nora Wieser
Juego Abierto

eran borrosos visitantes
extraños mensajeros de otro mundo
traían en su risa contenida las palabras
nunca dichas
con ojos de mirad͠ ͡etorno
tratando de mov͠ ͡s las cosas los lugares
usando la comida
haciéndose el amor entre sábanas dolidas
burlándose burlándose
burlándome
amenazadoramente vivos
de tan muertos.

Juego Abierto

they were nebulous visitors
strange messengers from another world
in their contained laughter they brought
never spoken words
their eyes with gazes of no return
trying to move all things out of place
using the food
making love between pained sheets
making fun, making fun
making fun of me
they were menacingly alive
from being so dead.

Translated by Nora Wieser
Juego Abierto

la forma pequeña forma
de que no me importe
si ponerme un sombrero
o salir a cantar
aunque no sólo
no sepa hacerlo
sino que no lo hago
válgame dios cómo puedo arreglar
la maraña
si no soy gato para ovillo
digo que no me gusta ser
primera persona a secas
prefiero el plural
pero cuando no hay vuelta
hay que agarrarse fuerte
para no tambalear ni un poquito.

Juego Abierto

the form small form
that to me it doesn't matter
if I put on a hat
or go out singing
even though not only
I don't know how
but I don't do it
good grief how to
straighten the mess
if I'm not a cat for
tangled threads
I say I don't like to be
first person cut and dry
I prefer the plural
but when there's no return
one has to grab hold firmly
so as not to stumble even a little.

Translated by Nora Wieser
Juego Abierto

último capítulo de una madurez
en ciernes
dijeron los ilustres
y yo me pregunto dónde están
los que ven la muerte a la orden del día
el hambre a plazo fijo
el derrumbe lento del orden establecido
dónde están los que hablan
de renuncias
y continúan en sus coitos sabatinos
la heladera y el tacón última moda
dónde humanidad Oh dulce dama
pervertida
y la madurez se viene galopando.

Juego Abierto

the last chapter of a maturity
in bloom
said the illustrious
and I ask myself
where are those who see death as the rhythm of each day
hunger in fixed installments
the slow destruction of established order
where are those who speak
of renouncements
and continue their Saturday coition
the refrigerator and latest heels in fashion
where humanity oh sweet perverted
lady
and maturity comes galloping.

Translated by Nora Wieser
Juego Abierto

te necesito
aquí y ahora
con todo el egoísmo del te amo
dejá todo y escuchame
que tengo que decirte
una bobada
que tengo que explicarte
que hoy se me rompió
otro pedacito
de cara.

Juego Abierto

I need you
here and now
with all the ego of I love you
drop everything and listen to me
I have to tell you
something silly
I have to explain to you
that today
another piece of my face
broke off.

Translated by Nora Wieser
Juego Abierto

BIBLIOGRAPHY OF WORKS IN ENGLISH

I.   **Research Bibliographies**
     A. Corvalan, Graciela. *Latin American Women Writers in English Translation.* (work in progress).
     B. Knoster, Meri. *Women in Spanish America. An Annotated Bibliography from Pre-Conquest to Contemporary Times.* Boston: G.K. Hall and Co., 1977, 696 pp.

II. **General Bibliography**
     Chase, Kathleen. "Latin American Women Writers: Their Present Position." *Books Abroad,* XXXIII (1959), pp. 150–151.
     Figueira, Gastón. "Daughters of the Muse." *Americas* (Nov., 1950), pp. 28–39. (It deals mainly with Uruguayan women writers.)
     Latin American Women Writers: Yesterday and Today. An Anthology. Special Issue edited by the *Latin American Literary Review.* Carnegie-Mellon University, Pittsburgh, 1977.
     Luisi, Luisa. "The Literature of Uruguay in the Year of its Constitutional Centenary." *Bulletin of the Pan American Union,* LXIV, 7 (July, 1930), pp. 655–695. (It studies some women poets such as M.E. Vaz Ferreira, D. Agustini, J. de Ibarbourou.)
     Rosenbaum, Sidonia. *Modern Women Poets of Spanish America. The Precursors: Delmira Agustini, Gabriela Mistral, Alfonsina Storni, Juana de Ibarbourou.* New York: Hispanic Institute, 1945.
     Zapata, Celia Correa de, "One Hundred Years of Women Writers in Latin America." *Latin American Literary Review,* III (Spring-Summer, 1975), pp. 7–16.

III. **Anthologies**
     Arciniegas, Germán, ed. *The Green Continent. A Comprehensive View of Latin America by its Leading Writers.* Translated from Spanish by Harriet de Onís and others. New York: Alfred A. Knopf, Inc., 1944, 533 pp. (Poems by Gabriela Mistral.)

Bankier Joanna, Earnschaw Doris and Lashgari, Deirdre, and others. *The Other Voice. Twentieth-Century Women's Poetry in Translation.* Foreword by A. Rich. New York: W.W. Norton and Co., Inc., 1976. (Poems by A. Storni, Cecilia Meireles, G. Mistral.)

Beck, Claudia and Carranza, Sylvia, eds. *Cuban Poetry, 1959-1966.* Foreword by Heberto Padilla and Luis Suardíaz. Havana, Cuba: Book Institute, 1967, 788 pp. (Belkis Cuza Malé)

Benedetti, Mario, ed. *Unstill Life. An Introduction to the Spanish Poetry of Latin America.* Translated by Darwin Flakoll and Claribel Alegría. Illustrated by Antonio Frasconi. New York: Harcourt, Brace and World, 1969, 127 pp. (Poems by Gabriela Mistral, A. Storni, Juana de Ibarbourou.)

Benson, Rachel, trans. *Nine Latin American Poets.* New York: Las Americas Publishing Co., 1968, 359 pp. (Poems by Alfonsina Storni.)

Bishop, Elizabeth and Brasil, Emanuel, eds. *An Anthology of Twentieth Century Brazilian Poetry.* Middleton, Conn.: Wesleyan University Press, 1972, 181 pp. (Poems by Cecilia Meireles.)

Blackwell, Alice Stone. *Some Spanish—American Poets.* Translated by Alice S. Blackwell; with an Introduction and Notes by Isaac Goldberg. Philadelphia: University of Pennsylvania Press, 1973, 2nd. ed. 1939, 559 pp. (Poems by G. Mistral, A. Storni, J. de Ibarbourou.)

Craig, G. Dundas. *The Modernist Trend in Spanish-American Poetry. A Collection of Representative Poems, the Modernist Movement and the Reaction.* Translated into English with a Commentary by Dunas G. Craig. Berkeley, California: University of California Press, 1937, 347 pp. (Poems by G. Mistral and A. Storni.)

Cranfill, Thomas Mabry, ed. *The Muse in Mexico. A Mid-Century Miscellany.* Translations and editing by George D. Schade. Austin: University of Texas Press, 1959, 177 pp. (Poems by Rosario Castellanos.)

Fitts, Dudley, ed. *Anthology of Contemporary Latin American Poetry.* Norfolk, Conn.: A New Directions Book, 1942., 1947, 677 pp. (Poems by Claudia Lars, A. Storni, J. de Ibarbourou, G. Mistral.)

275

Flakoll, Darwin J. and Alegría, Claribel. *New Voices of Hispanic America. An Anthology.* Boston: Beacon Press, 1962, 226 pp. (Poems by R. Castellanos.)

Flores, Angel, ed. and various translators. *An Anthology of Spanish Poetry from Garcilaso to Lorca.* In English translation with Spanish originals. Garden City, N.Y.: Anchor Books, 1961, 561 pp. (Poems by G. Mistral.)

Gannon, Patricio, and Manning, Hugo. *Argentine Anthology of Modern Verse.* Buenos Aires: Ed. Francisco A. Colombo, 1942, 77 pp. (Poems by A. Storni.)

Johnson, Mildred E., trans. and ed. *Spanish Poems of Love.* New York: Exposition Press, 1955. (Poems by J. de Ibarbourou and A. Storni.)

Johnson, Mildred E. *Swan, Cignets and Owl, An Anthology of Modernist Poetry in Spanish America.* Columbia, Missouri: The University of Missouri Studies, 1959, (volume XXIX), 199 pp.. (Poems by D. Agustini and Juana de Ibarbourou.)

Jones, Willis Knapp. *Spanish American Literature in Translation: A Selection of Prose, Poetry and Drama since 1888.* Volume II. New York: Frederick Ungar Publishing Co., 1966. (Poems by Claudia Lars, G. Mistral, A. Storni.)

Nist, John, ed. and Trans. *Modern Brazilian Poetry. An Anthology.* Bloomington: Indiana University Press, 1962, 175 pp. (Poems by Cecilia Meireles.)

Patterson, Helen Wohl. *Poetizas de América.* (A bilingual anthology). Washington, D.C.: The Mitchell Press, 1960, 217 pp.

Resnik, Seymour. *Spanish-American Poetry. A Bilingual Selection.* Irvington-On-Hudson, New York: Harvey House, Inc., 1964, 96 pp. (Poems by J. de Ibarbourou, G. Mistral, and A. Storni.)

Shand, William. *Contemporary Argentine Poetry.* An Anthology Compiled and Translated by William Shand. Introduction by Aldo Pelegrini. Buenos Aires: Fundación Argentina para la Poesía, 1969, 275 pp. (Poems by A. Pizarnik, Olga Orozco.)

Tarn, Nathaniel, ed. *Con Cuba. An Anthology of Cuban Poetry of the Last Sixty Years.* London: Cape Goliard Press, in Association with Grossman Publishers, New York, 1969, 142 pp. (Poems by B. Cuza Malé.)

Translations from Hispanic Poets. New York: Hispanic Society of America, 1938, 271 pp. (Poems by A. Storni, J. de Ibarbourou, G. Mistral.)

Trend, J.B. *Modern Poetry from Brazil.* Cambridge, Great Britain: R.I. Severs, Ltd., 1955, 32 pp. (Poems by Cecilia Meireles.)

Veríssimo, Erico. *Brazilian Literature: An Outline.* New York: The MacMillan Co., 1945, 184 pp. (Poems by C. Meireles.)

Young Poetry of the Americas. Volume I. Washington, D.C.: Pan American Union, 1967, 116 pp. (Poems by Claudia Lars, Eunice Odio.)

IV. **Selected Critical Works for Specific Women Poets in the Anthology**
  1. Delmira Agustini

     Stephens, Doris T. "Delmira Agustini and the Quest for Transcendence." Unpublished Dissertation. University of Tennesse, 1974.

     Valenti, Jeanette Y. de Guzmán. "Delmira Agustini: A Reinterpretation of her Poetry." Unpublished Ph.D. Dissertation. Cornell University, 1971.

  2. Juana de Ibarbourou

     Luisi, Luisa. "Two South American Poets: Gabriela Mistral and Juana de Ibarbourou." *Bulletin of the Pan American Union,* 64, No. 1 (June 1930), pp. 588–590.

  3. Cecilia Meireles

     García, Rubén Victor. "Modernity and Tradition in Cecilia Meireles." Unpublished Doctoral Dissertation, University of Texas at Austin, 1975.

     Nist, John. "The Poetry of Cecilia Meireles." *Hispania,* 46 (May 1963), pp. 252–258.

     Sayer, Raymond. "The Brazilian Woman Poet in the Twentieth Century: Cecilia Meireles." In *Homenaje a Andrés Iduarte,* ofrecido por sus amigos y discípulos. Clear Creek, Indiana: American Hispanist, 419 pp., pp. 361–370.

  4. Gabriela Mistral

     Selected Poems of Gabriela Mistral. Trans. and Annotated by Doris Dana. Foreword by Francisco Aguilera and Introduction by Margaret Bates. Baltimore: The Library of the Congress by the Johns Hopkins Press, 1961, 235 pp.

Selected Poems by Gabriela Mistral. Translation and Introduction by Langston Hughes. Bloomington, Indiana: Indiana University Press, 1957, 119 pp.

Arce de Vázquez, Margot. *Gabriela Mistral, the Poet and Her Work.* Transl. by H. Masslo Anderson. New York: New York University Press, 1964, 158 pp.

Bates, Margaret J. "Apropos an Article on Gabriela Mistral." *The Americas,* 14, 2 (1957), pp. 145-151.

Caimano, Sister Rose Aquín. "Mysticism in Gabriela Mistral: A Clarification." Unpublished Doctoral Dissertation, St. Johns University, Jamaica, New York, 1957.

Cord, William Owen. "The Major Themes in the Poetry of Gabriela Mistral." Unpublished M.A. Thesis, Washington University, St. Louis, 1948.

Gabriela Mistral, 1889-1957. Washington, D.C.: Pan American Union, 1958. (Content: five essays in Spanish on Gabriela Mistral and a very good bibliography by Albanell and Nancy Mango.

Pane, Remigio Ugo. "Gabriela Mistral: (Lucila Godoy Alcayaga), Chile, b. 1889: A Bibliography of her poems in English Translation together with a list of her Works," *Bulletin of Bibliography and Drama Index,* 18, 5 (Sept.-Dec. 1944), p. 104-105.

Peers, E. Allison. "Gabriela Mistral: A Tentative Evaluation," *Bulletin of Spanish Studies* (Liverpool, Institute of Hispanic Studies), 23 (1946), pp. 101-116.

Portes, Grace Marie. "Gabriela Mistral: A Study of Motherhood in her Prose and Poetry." Unpublished M.A. Thesis. New York: Columbia University Press, 1947.

Preston, Sister M. Charles Anne. *A Study of Significant Variants in the Poetry of Gabriela Mistral.* Ph.D. Diss. Washington, D.C.: The Catholic University of America, Studies in Romance Languages and Literatures, vol. LXX, 1964.

Rudd, Margaret T. *Gabriela Mistral—The Chilean Years.* Alabama: University of Alabama Press, 1968.

Taylor, Martin C. *Gabriela Mistral's Religious Sensibility.* Berkeley: University of California Press, 1968.

5. Alfonsina Storni

Munk Benton, Gabriele von. "Recurring Themes in Alfonsina Storni's Poetry." *Hispania*, XXXIII, no. 2, (May 1959), pp. 151–153.

Phillips, Rachel. *Alfonsina Storni, From Poetess to Poet*. London: Tamesis Books Limited, 1975.

Titiev, Janine Geasler. "Alfonsina Storni's *Mundo de siete pozos*: Form, Freedom and Fantasy." *Kentucky Romance Quarterly*, 23, pp. 185–197.